UNIQUE INTERIORS IN MINUTES

UNIQUE INTERIORS

IN MINUTES

STEWART WALTON AND ELIZABETH WILHIDE

Chilton Book Company
Radnor, Pennsylvania

First published in the UK in 1993 as
Instant Decorating by
Conran Octopus Limited
37 Shelton Street, London WC2H 9HN

First published in the United States
of America by
Chilton Book Company, Radnor,
Pennsylvania 19089

Library of Congress Catalog Card No:
92–54913

ISBN 0–8019–8480–7

Typeset by Servis Filmsetting
Limited, Manchester
Manufactured in Hong Kong

Project Editor *Simon Willis*
Editorial Assistant *Michael Williams*
Americanizer *Christine Rickerby*

Art Editor *Helen Lewis*
Illustrations *Lynne Robinson*
Stewart Walton
Picture Researcher *Jessica Walton*

Production Controller *Jill Macey*

PUBLISHER'S ACKNOWLEDGMENTS

The publisher would like to thank the following for their assistance with this book: Michelle Clark; Dylon; Matthew Usmar Lauder; and Mathers and Powell, London.

Special thanks to **Arthur Sanderson and Sons Ltd, London** for supplying the paint used in the special projects.

INTRODUCTION

INTRODUCTION

Everyone knows how creating a beautiful home is supposed to be: painstaking preparation with layer upon layer of undercoat; silky smooth finishes sanded and honed to perfection; expertly lined and weighted drapery with intricate hand sewing; professionally tailored upholstery with all the trimmings; and delightful displays of well-chosen, recherché *objects. The exquisite and tasteful result will reflect a lifetime's diligent application.*

Decorating can seem terribly intimidating. Judging by the wealth of publications pouring forth advice and glossy images, it can also be hideously expensive and exceptionally time-consuming. At the very least, you will need a degree in art history and a diploma in advanced Do It Yourself to bring your own four walls up to an acceptable standard of taste and finish. Unlimited funds, all the free time in the world and a charming period property will also come in handy.

The truth, thankfully, is very different. The secret of successful decorating, as many people are increasingly aware, is neither time, nor money, nor specialized skills – but imagination. Some of the most exciting and original effects are the results of flashes of inspiration hastily executed on a wet Sunday afternoon, or brilliant exercises in lateral thinking that cross-fertilize ideas, techniques and materials from different disciplines in a sudden burst of innovation and creativity.

This book is for those people with little time and money, but who want to bring sparkle to the dull corners of their homes. It is for new home owners confronting blank spaces with little spare change in their pockets; students who want to give their rented apartment a facelift; those whose time for Do It Yourself is only as long as a baby's nap; or those whose enthusiasm flags at the second undercoat. It is for those who vow to do it "properly"... one *day.*

Cheap and Cheerful

If you can't afford to replaster walls to create an immaculately smooth surface for decorating, exploit the textural effect of a rough finish. This uneven pink-painted wall has a forthright style – beautiful in its own right (left)**. Paint supplies the suggestion of architectural detail in the form of simple freehand wainscotting** (right)**.**

The scolding tone of much decorating advice makes departing from the straight and narrow seem risky. But what such worthy professionalism conceals is that taking shortcuts is itself a professional approach. Photographic stylists and set designers conjure bravura effects with simple techniques and materials. And there are plenty of interior decorators whose best efforts owe more to an impetuous moment than a lifetime's expertise.

There is room for both approaches. But there is a time in most people's lives when resources are stretched and instant decorating is the only alternative to none at all. And for those wedded to textbook methods, the instant approach is a reminder that decorating can – and should – be fun.

GETTING STARTED

SOURCES OF IDEAS

The instant decorator can take heart that many decorative effects and even some historical styles owe a great deal to a spirit of improvisation. In the past, when materials were rare, expensive or hard to come by, people had to make do with what was to hand and the robust, exuberant results of this approach often seem more vital and appealing today than the virtuoso displays of fine craftsmanship in more stately surroundings.

Early colonists, for example, working to establish their settlements in hard conditions, had little leisure and no money to import expensive luxuries such as hand-printed wallpapers from Europe. Instead, using colored limewash, earth colors, and even soot, they stenciled their own simple hand-cut patterns directly onto walls or paneling, over fireplaces and on furniture, a vivacious and free interpretation of the rhythm and structure of traditional wallpaper designs. And in some cases, paint was daubed on freehand in remarkable splodges and graphic blots – revealing with an endearing directness a deep desire for decoration whatever the limits of present circumstances.

Away from European folk court circles and grand country houses, such ingenious economies were usual. Vernacular traditions of decoration sometimes copied in cheaper materials what might be finely executed in luxury ones, but equally often displayed their own forthright style of decoration, handed down through generations. Rough walls washed in brilliant color or chalky white, homespun textiles set off with the simplest trimming, quilts and rugs pieced with scraps and snips of fabric, stylized natural or geometric patterns, and the soothing harmonies of stone and wood and clay are the basic elements we have fashioned into country style today: an instant vocabulary of simple, cheap decoration.

Around the world many of these folk traditions persist, a source of ideas for every instant decorator. Paint, easy to use and cheap, is the basis for much decorative gaiety. Along the shores of the Mediterranean and Caribbean, brilliant partnerships of white, sea greens and blues, hot pinks and rich ochers underscore architectural detail, singing out on painted shutters and doors. Zig zag patterning inside an African mud hut, the scorching clash of pink and magenta on a Mexican verandah, dashing pillarbox red window frames and whitewashed walls on an Irish cottage are examples that vividly illustrate simple means of enrichment.

Art is another potent inspiration, whether it takes the form of calligraphic squiggles and dots painted freehand on the wall for a Matisse-like background; Cocteau-inspired flights of fancy with mirror, fake leopardskin, and voluminous drapery; or solid blocks of primary color for Mondrian modernism.

All kinds of "found" objects, beautiful and free, can be the basis for a decorative theme. Sea shells piled in a glass jar or ranged on a window sill are a popular form of display; or you could go further and use the shells as decoration, sticking them on to a mantelpiece or threading them on to muslin curtains. Similarly, packing trunks could be revamped as seating or low tables; battered baskets, waterings-cans, and buckets all make excellent containers.

One piece of advice often given in decorating books is to keep a scrapbook of ideas: pages torn from magazines, postcards, scraps of fabric or ribbon – anything which attracts you for its color, pattern, or ingenuity. This may feel wincingly self-conscious at first, but it will help you decide what you really like and will build up a fund of ideas to spark your imagination. More importantly, it can save a great deal of time when you are trying to think what to do with the spare room and your mind goes suddenly blank.

Favorite Things

An essential element of instant decorating is the display of favorite things. A collection of figures and animals is set off by a vivid turquoise background (opposite above).

Authentic Decor

There is a good historic precedent for painting wooden furniture (opposite below).

Seashore

A beachcomber's treasure trove is a fine example of "themed" improvisation.

PREPARATION

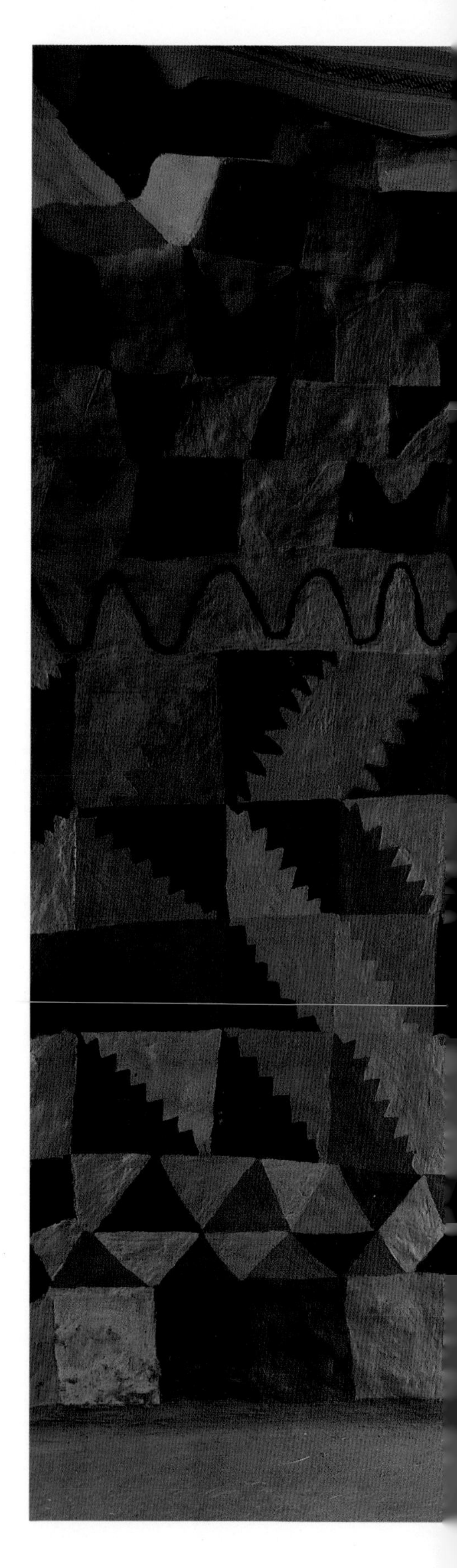

Before you begin, it is wise to be aware of what instant decorating can't do. It goes without saying that no amount of decorating, instant or otherwise, is going to correct the effects of serious structural faults (the kind that result in large cracks, sagging floors, and seeping damp stains), although some superficial concealment may be possible. Really poor surfaces – pitted, holed, and cracked – will only be hidden by sticking a layer of something else – such as paper, fabric, or wood – over the top. The dull truth is that sound, time-consuming preparation is necessary for smooth, even finishes, sharp corners and true edges.

Instant decorating is not a strategy for perfection or a panacea for all decorating ills, but it is a way of using shortcuts and sideways jumps to make the most of limited resources. It is unlikely that your starting point will be a perfectly prepared surface: and if not, the end product won't be either. But it will be lively, cheerful and infinitely more pleasing to live with than it was before.

How little basic preparation you can get away with is a critical issue, and is something that manufacturers are constantly addressing with their ranges of one-coat paints, non-drip solid latex, and quick-drying varnishes. Modern paint covers a multitude of sins: on walls you can assume that hairline cracks and small irregularities will be less noticeable and that general griminess will disappear after a coat or two. For gloss-painted or varnished woodwork, a little sanding is all that is required to provide a key for a new coat of paint. And if a country look is what you're after, painted furniture often looks more authentically rustic if the cracks aren't all filled or the imperfections sanded away.

Provided that the cracks are not crevices, the irregularities are not craters and the baseboard moldings are not clogged with layers of tacky gloss, basic repainting will freshen and improve any

African Zig zag

The urge to decorate one's surroundings is universal, transcending limitations of material and circumstance. Bravura patterning transforms the walls of an African mud house. Bold chevrons, zig zags, and toothed edging carried out in the warm palette of natural earth colors – terra cotta, rust, rich brown, and buff – express a tribal exuberance.

surface immeasurably for just a small amount of time and trouble. One proviso is that you do not try to save money by choosing cheap paint: it does not cover well, so more coats are needed; it streaks and smears, so color is uneven. Don't ever be tempted to pry open a can of paint and slap it straight on without first brushing down the surface to remove loose dirt and dust, or without covering yourself and adjacent surfaces to protect against spills and splashes.

The same holds true for other aspects of instant decorating. Spend a few minutes assembling whatever tools and materials you will need to complete the job, move furniture out of the way if necessary and cover up what you can't move. A few minutes spent being sensible and organized at the outset will save you hours trying to get paint out of the carpet or glue off the upholstery later on.

BENDING THE RULES

Instant decoration really comes into its own in the use of materials and tools. Hardware stores are stacked with dozens of brushes for every conceivable application, together with impossibly technical-looking tools and equipment with little indication as to their ultimate purpose. For the confused amateur, such displays are as likely to sap confidence as to empty the wallet.

The list of basic tools you will need to complete most decorating jobs is actually quite short. Good paintbrushes are essential: wide for tackling large surface areas and narrow for trims and details. Rollers speed up large painting jobs, and foam rollers can be cut to create instant special effects. Ordinary artists' brushes – synthetic will do just as well as sable – are ideal for adding fine decorative detail. Pencils, a ruler, and tracing-paper are needed for setting out stencil patterns and other preparatory work, while masking tape saves time in cutting around trim and details.

Many accessories can be improvised from what you already have around the home. A bucket or old roasting pan serves as a receptacle for paint; old saucepans or large jars are useful for mixing colors. An old plate makes a good palette for mixing shades for decorative details. Spare rolls of plain lining paper or wooden scraps are invaluable for trying out ideas.

Paint effects are essentially improvised – the result of decorators trying out different materials and tools in order to achieve a particular result. Old rags, kitchen cloths, chamois leathers, bathroom sponges, toothbrushes, nailbrushes, household brushes, and brooms are just some of the ad-hoc *tools that have been used to create the dappled, stippled, and streaked color effects that have become so fashionable in recent years. You can buy an expensive stippling brush from a specialist decorators' suppliers, but if a cut-down household brush does the job, why spend the money?*

You may, however, like to invest in a number of tools not normally associated with traditional decorating. A staple gun, for example, is necessary for some of the "soft-furnishing" projects described in this book. Glue guns are another standby of set design and window display which also have a place in instant decoration. Spray painting is, naturally, quicker than brush-painting, and can transform techniques such as stenciling. Other tools and materials mentioned during the course of this book are no more obscure than colored felt-tipped pens or upholstery tacks.

As far as paint is concerned, latex (water-based) paint is better for basic decoration than oil-based paints such as eggshell or gloss, even for painting furniture. Latex is quick-drying and with a pleasing finish that recalls the chalkiness of old-fashioned, home-made paints; its spills and splashes are also much easier and less time-consuming to clean up afterwards.

All White

A monochromatic palette simplifies decorating decisions and effortlessly creates a mood of serene sophistication. Chairs wrapped in white sheeting acquire a mysterious presence of their own – an economical, washable, and easily renewed form of covering when new upholstery would break the budget.

QUICK
QUAKER
OATS
BREAD BOOK

Covering Up

Covering Up

Tackling large surface areas – walls, ceilings, and floors – is usually a daunting prospect. But even if resources are limited, it is worth getting the background right, as any improvement here will have a beneficial effect on the whole room.

Backgrounds don't have to be boring. The purpose of many paint effects and techniques is to create a quiet, shimmering surface with a pattern, texture, or subtle modulation of color that gives depth and atmosphere. It is usually a good idea to keep walls, ceilings, and floors fairly low key, and then to splash intense spots of color on furnishings, pictures, or objects.

Braver souls may still find it hard to resist a bold approach. Walls drenched in strong color can have an unbeatable vitality that lifts any room out of the ordinary, but it takes a sure touch to keep all the elements under control.

Whichever strategy you adopt, take a cold hard look at the basic features of the room before you begin. What is worth enhancing, and which aspects need to be disguised? You may want to supply architectural distinction in the form of a paper frieze or a painted or stenciled pattern at cornice height. Awkward angles and irregularities can be dissolved with a flowing, all-over pattern, while if surfaces are simply too poor to paint, consider covering them completely using paper or fabric.

Attention to detail is often taken as a way of urging perfection, and perfection is often what the instant decorator cannot afford. Even small items can cost a surprising amount. If you have to be economical you can devote your efforts to the details that really make a difference, and save worrying about the rest until later.

Fast Work

Simple all-over patterns quickly cover large areas. Try stenciling gold stars over a midnight-blue background (above)**. Graphic blots daubed on a white wall show how early American settlers utilized basic materials** (right)**, while freehand dots and a painted frieze provide a mellow background** (far right)**.**

COLOR

Colorways

The decoration here makes a virtue out of necessity, picking out angles and planes in different colors. This bold strategy helps to compensate for the lack of fine architectural detail (far right)**.**

Instant Wainscotting

Wainscotting is traditionally covered in a different material from the wall above. In default of paneling or textured paper, this wainscotting makes use of lines and squiggles, cross hatched in paint (above)**.**

Once you have worked out a basic strategy for redecorating your room, the next decision is likely to concern color. As far as interiors are concerned, most of us have had our ideas on color shaped by the marketing departments of paint manufacturers. We are accustomed to thinking in terms of color cards, those sheets of innumerable tinted squares that seem to offer every possibility but are in reality so intimidating and inhibiting.

In practice, by far the best way to understand the power and potential of color is to forget about color cards altogether and to experiment with color mixing yourself. In this you can be guided by the advice that art teachers generally give their students: namely, to start with a limited palette and build up a thorough appreciation of all the subtle half-shades and mixtures that can be achieved using only a small selection of colors.

The most basic form of color mixing is simply to add a tint to white. A spoonful of color mixed into a can of white latex will give you the same type of tinted white that is enthusiastically promoted by paint companies. The color that you add to the latex base can consist of anything, provided that it is water-soluble: more latex, colored ink, gouache (opaque watercolor), food, or fabric dye – even cold coffee or turmeric. It is worth experimenting with "found" color to create unusual shades. The one basic rule that you must follow is that water-based products can be mixed and oil-based products (such as gloss paint, eggshell, undercoat, and artists' oils) can be mixed, but oil and water never mix.

As well as creating new colors, you can also achieve really interesting

textures. Mixing opaque paint and transparent varnish in the ratio of about one part paint to ten parts varnish, for example, results in a milky finish similar to limewash once it has dried and been rubbed back using steel wool or a scrub brush.

This type of one-step color mixing is ideal for creating a single color or texture. Going a stage further, mixing two complementary colors and white will give you a family of related shades, enough to develop the basis of an interesting decorative scheme.

Color theory can take you into the abstruse realms of optics and applied psychology. For decorative purposes, it is enough to understand that each color has an opposite or complementary color. Red is paired with green, blue with orange, and yellow with purple. When these pairs are used together in their pure, intense forms the result is electric and vibrant. This "chemistry" of color relationships is exploited in all of the most successful contemporary decorating schemes.

You can see how the process works by choosing two complementaries and trying out different combinations. If you choose a red and a green, for example, they may not be perfectly matched in tone or intensity. But if you mix a small quantity of the green into the red and a small quantity of the red into the green, the two new colors will automatically be linked. To take the mixture a shade lighter, add white; to darken it, add more of the complementary color. If you continue the process of mixing the colors in different ratios, you will eventually build up a whole family of related colors, from pastels to murky tones, all of which will work well together in a room.

SURFACE DESIGN

Classical Stripe

Tented rooms decorated in striped fabric were the height of fashion in early nineteenth-century Europe. A hint of this military style is achieved using broad chalky blue stripes painted on the wall and by the simply draped metal bedstead (above).

Paint effects are ideal for instant decoration. Many of these improvised techniques evolved as ways of imitating something too expensive to use, notably marble, granite, and other luxurious materials. Spattering, sponging, stippling, ragging, and graining may sound like esoteric branches of the decorator's art, but in fact they are nothing more than ways of making textured paint marks or patterns on a surface such as a wall or ceiling.

In the realm of paint finishes, it is easy to become obsessed with different methods and recipes, tools and paint mixtures. But what really counts is achieving the finish you want, not how you get there. You can work freehand if that proves more effective, or use a combination of methods or tools. If you forget about recipes and concentrate on the process of pattern making, you may surprise yourself with an interesting result you hadn't anticipated.

Experiment with different household brushes, rags, sponges, and scraps of fabric, dipping each in paint and testing the print in a sheet of lining paper to see which effect you like best. Cut up foam rollers to make instant stripes, or cut sponges into shapes for printing. Scrub brushes can be cut as well to make a ragged, non-mechanical striping similar to graining.

What most of these methods have in common is that they produce a broken-color finish in which the base coat shows through a patterned top layer. For the amateur, it is best to keep the top coat close in tone and color to the

Borders

Photocopied leaf-prints trim a striped paint effect made from a cut roller (above).

Subtle tones

Paint effects are often best in subtle near-shades, such as pale yellow on white. For the amateur, mistakes will be less obvious and the final effect more sophisticated than bold contrasts. Broad stripes can be painted easily and quickly using paint rollers – vary the size according to the width you require (above).

base coat. This is because success with these techniques relies on the ability to cover the ground consistently and evenly; and so if the two colors are closely related, then mistakes and smudges will be less obvious.

Color washing with a weak solution of water-based paint is a quick way of adding some instant color or modifying an unattractive wall shade. You can tone down an egg yellow, for example, with sweeping strokes of diluted red on a large brush, without losing the essential warmth of the original shade. The obvious brushmarks that result from this method are part of the charm of the finish. In general, it obviously saves time if you can work with an existing background in this way, rather than repainting it completely. This is especially true if the wall is dark in tone, as several light-colored coats would be needed to cover it up.

Color washing is also one of the techniques that can be used to age a surface artificially. It may seem positively perverse to go to the trouble of simulating the effects of wear and decay, but what professionals like to call the "patina of age" can be very appealing. Ageing a surface by washing it with several related earth tones, or creating crazed or crackled effects with flecks of undercolor, can result in finishes with great depth and character. Making a virtue of imperfections is easier than starting from scratch, and these mellow yet lively backgrounds are less demanding of perfection than other areas of decoration.

Textured Paint

These broad textured panels, crisply defined by areas of plain paint, make an interesting variation on a striped theme. The distressed effect can be achieved by removing flecks and patches of wet paint with a dry roller (above).

PAINTED PLAID

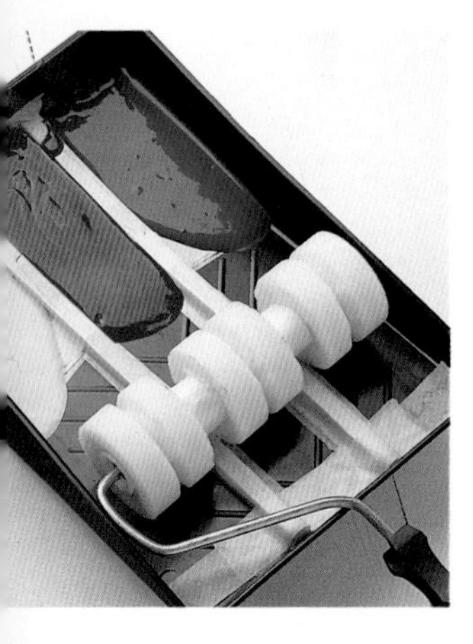

Tartan Roller

Cut a paint roller into three equal sections, binding masking tape in between to keep them separate. Then tie each section in half with string. Divide a paint tray into sections corresponding to the cuts in the roller; use strips of plastic or batten secured with waterproof tape (above). **Fill each section with a different color. Add water if the paint is too thick. Roller the verticals first, lining up by eye with the corner of the wall. Wait about ten minutes, then roller the horizontals.**

Oil and Water

Paint falls into two main categories: water-based (latex) and oil-based (gloss, eggshell, and undercoat). Water-based paints are thinned with water and can be colored by adding any other water-soluble paint or substance (watercolor paints, acrylic, gouache). Oil-based paints are thinned with turpentine and can be colored using artist's oil paints. But remember that oil and water don't mix.

Paint Effects

Color washes

A tinted wash can be applied over any water-based painted background. The basic recipe is water and acrylic varnish in the ratio of about 2:1. Mix up a little water-based color – watercolor, inks, gouache – to a thin, creamy consistency and test the color before adding to the wash. A wash with less water has more body.

Zig Zag Paint

This zig zag effect is created with a proprietary paint pad cut to shape with a sharp knife and daubed randomly over a flat painted background. Test out prints first on scraps of paper to achieve the effect you want (left)**.**

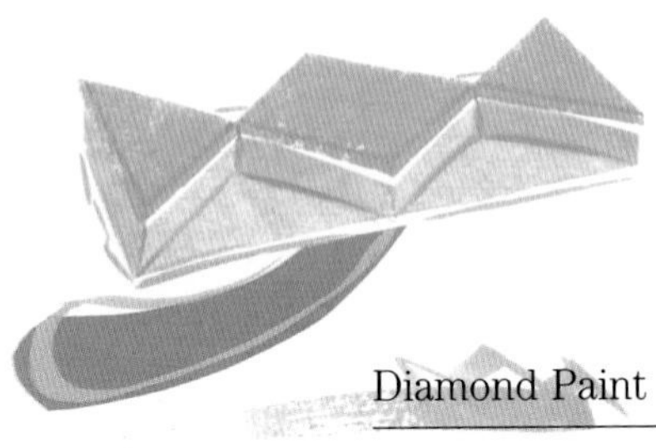

Diamond Paint

A rugged all-over diamond print is the result of using a paint pad cut as shown above, applied in vertical bands across a background. Textured rollers, of the type used to apply "artex" finishes, can also be worth trying out (right)**.**

Brushwork

Paintbrushes can be cut and shaped to make bold patterns in paint (left). **An ordinary decorator's brush is cut into three sections to make a randomly applied finish. These effects often work particularly well when background and foreground colors are similar in tone.**

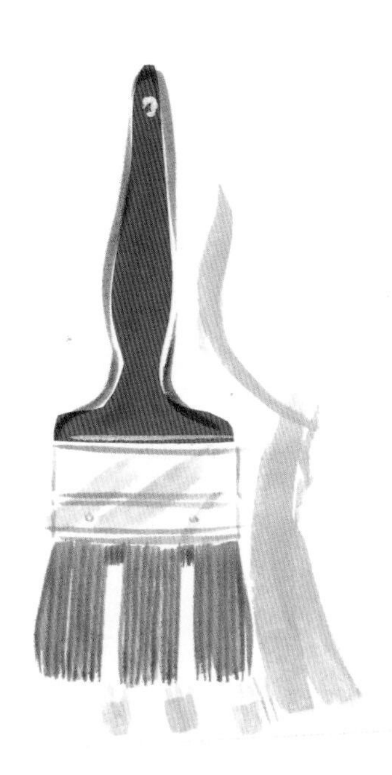

Glazes

Oil-based glazes take longer to dry than washes, and spills are more difficult to clear up. But the glowing, luminous effect can repay the extra effort. Turpentine is mixed with oil-based varnish in the proportions of 2:1, and add oil-based color to suit. Reducing the amount of solvent (turps) will create a glaze that has more body.

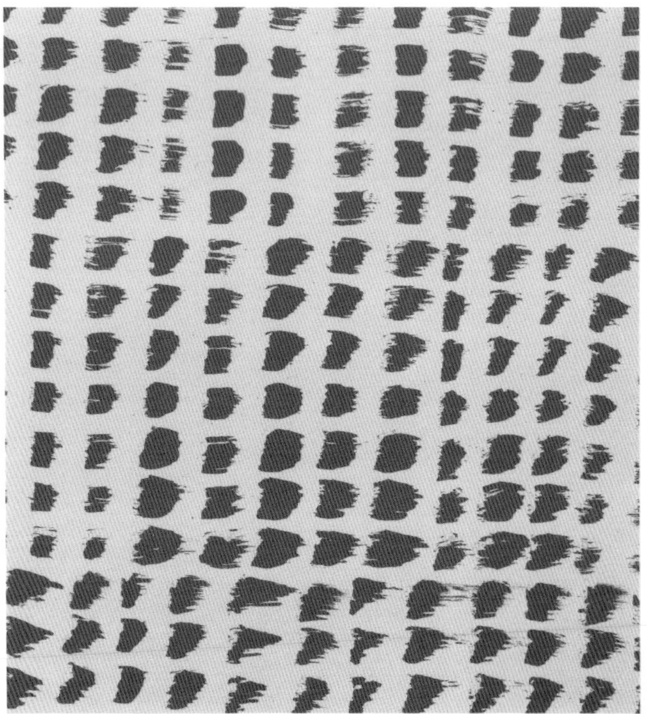

Checkerboard

A paperhanger's brush, normally used to apply wallpaper paste, is wide enough to allow a series of "teeth" to be cut. Experiment with paint consistency and pattern spacing to find the right effect (left).

PAPERING OVER

Some surfaces are beyond cosmetic improvement and require more radical measures. Covering up the offending wall or walls is one option that falls within the scope of the instant decorator. Lining walls with fabric requires patience and a degree of skill; although such transformations are highly effective, they are by no means instant, while wallpaper for a large room can be expensive. The answer is to look for inspiration in cheap sources of paper and other collage materials.

With ordinary wallpaper paste and a willingness to experiment, you can paper a wall with almost anything. Pages from comics, sheets of newspaper, maps, menus, playbills, sheets of music, gift wrap, Japanese or Chinese calligraphy all produce lively and graphic all-over patterning. This type of treatment should be used with discretion, but works particularly well in a small room such as a study or downstairs bathroom, rather than on large expanses of wall.

For a more sober effect, brown wrapping paper can make a surprisingly elegant background. Cheap textured papers (such as the kind often used by florists to wrap flowers) are equally good, or you could collage torn layers of fine colored tissue, sealed with a coat of varnish for protection. A photocopier is also a useful tool if you want to recreate the look of the traditional print room, with its cut-out enrichments and engravings stuck directly on to a subtly colored background.

Scrim

Scrim, the open woven mesh used by plasterers to seal the joints between plasterboard, is an unlikely choice for decorating, but the bold texture of this cheap and commonplace material acquires an intriguing look when pasted on a wall (right)**.**

Newspaper

The vertical emphasis of columns of newsprint shows how the daily newspaper can stand in splendidly for wallpaper. Use wallpaper paste sparingly, so as not to soak the paper, and take care to align columns of text as accurately as possible. An instant finishing touch is provided by a zig zag frieze of corrugated paper stenciled with a basic flower shape (right)**.**

PAUL McCARTNEY
La nuit sur la Cinq
LE CARNET DES BONNES AFFAIRES
IMMOBILIER DU FIGARO
XM V6
CITROËN
4 DERNIERS JOURS!

MAPPING IT OUT

Map Reading

All kinds of maps, navigation charts, and star guides make interesting substitutes for wallpaper. The two approaches shown here illustrate the range of possibilities. The patched assembly of individual old faded maps and charts makes a muted background for a study area (left)**, while a children's room has been papered in an educational and eye-catching large-scale world map** (right)**. When using any printed material to cover the walls, bear in mind that words written in your own language inevitably draw the eye and invite you to read what they say, while foreign language sources are less immediately recognizable and are consequently less insistent.**

SIGNED AND SEALED

Cut and Paste

Antique title deeds and other handwritten documents which turn up in junk-shops can provide the raw material for papering a wall. Here, photocopies of the same bond have been used to cover the wall of a study. Apply wallpaper paste to each sheet, stick in position, and brush out any air bubbles with a sponge or paintbrush. When the prints have dried in place, apply a thin coat of water-based tinted varnish to give an antique appearance. Apply the varnish unevenly with a medium-sized paintbrush; if the result is not dark enough, wait an hour and apply a second coat.

This Indenture

Sourcebook

The images shown on these two pages, all of which are out of copyright, make good starting points for photocopied effects. Use the copier to enlarge, reduce, and multiply; you can experiment with friezes, borders, or repeat patterning.

Questions of Scale

Headed Paper

Classically inspired, this black-and-white wallpaper features alternately large- and small-scale heads of Roman emperors (left)**. The effect recalls traditional print rooms with their cut-out engravings pasted onto the wall. A similar look could be achieved by photocopying and cutting out a favorite image in two different sizes to repeat around the room.**

Figure Frieze

Imitate the boldness of this expensive wallpaper by montaging photocopies of historical characters onto a wall. Reproduction medallions stuck to the wall provide a bold architectural frieze (left)**. Use the photocopier to make enlargements for all-over papering, good for lampshades as well as the wall** (above)**.**

ARCHITECTURAL DETAIL

If unsympathetic remodeling has stripped away all the architectural detail in a room – the cornices, brackets, architraves, medallions, and so on – it is relatively straightforward to reintroduce at least some of them. Reproductions of classic moldings and embellishments are widely available, either in plaster (which can be expensive), or in cheap, lightweight styrofoam. Although styrofoam versions sound cheap and nasty, they are very easy to install and, once up on the wall and painted, look surprisingly convincing. The plainer styles with simple profiles are generally best.

Wooden molding is versatile. A strip of beading will neatly cover any gap that may have opened up between baseboard molding and floor. Molding can be applied high up the wall as a picture-rail, or just under halfway down as wainscotting, although it is meaningless to add the latter if you don't then go on to treat the lower portion of the wall differently with paint, paper, or paneling. As long as you are using the molding simply to provide a decorative form of punctuation, you can simply glue it in place using an aliphatic resin adhesive although nailing it will give a more permanent result.

Star Panels

The effect of paneling can be created at a fraction of the cost by applying ready-made wooden moldings to the wall and treating the enclosed areas in a simple decorative way, as here with its bright stenciled stars (left).

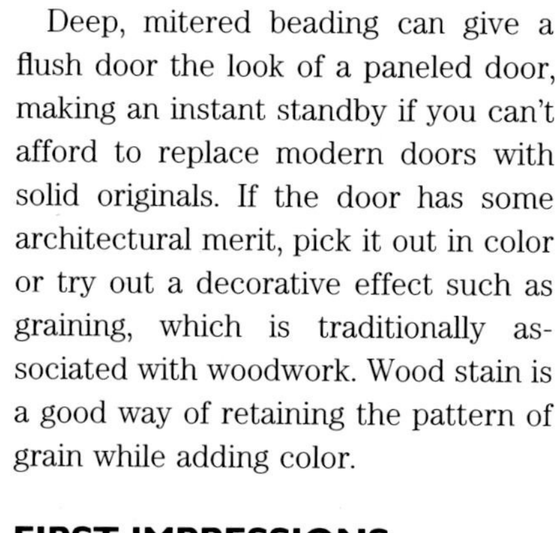

Deep, mitered beading can give a flush door the look of a paneled door, making an instant standby if you can't afford to replace modern doors with solid originals. If the door has some architectural merit, pick it out in color or try out a decorative effect such as graining, which is traditionally associated with woodwork. Wood stain is a good way of retaining the pattern of grain while adding color.

FIRST IMPRESSIONS

In the wider scheme of things, halls and entrances count as detail. It's easy enough to exhaust your creativity and your cash on the living room or kitchen and neglect to improve the area just past the front door at all. But while you won't spend much time there, the hall has a disproportionately large effect on the way both you and your visitors are likely to feel about your home, easing the transition from outdoors to in.

To begin with, a hall should give some kind of flavor or hint of what is to come, either through its color or decorative effect. Strong, positive color is often avoided in hallways and on stairs because people think it can limit color choices in the rooms opening on to these connecting areas.

Very little in the way of furniture will fit into the average hall; in any case, clutter is best kept to a minimum. A narrow table is a good place for the mail – better than piling it all in a heap on the stairs – as well as for a jug of flowers, making a refreshing sight for everyone coming and going during the day. Even if your front hall furniture is limited to a telephone table and a chair, some sort of punctuation point is better than a featureless corridor.

Architrave

Lateral thinking is called for when you need to compensate for a lack of good architectural detail. You can add interest to what would otherwise be featureless door-ways by painting the inner surfaces of plain doorways in a distinctive color (right)**.**

Stairway

The simple device of outlining a stair with a strip of contrasting color makes up for the absence of defining moldings or trim (above)**. The same strategy can be used to paint in a baseboard molding or to frame a doorway.**

PICKING OUT

Sea View

A deeply recessed window is given extra definition by a border of starfish, stuck straight onto the rough plastered wall. The marine display in the window recess reinforces the theme (right).

A quick way to transform a room is to add colored or patterned detail around the margins. Friezes, borders, and painted banding all inject a graphic quality to the decoration, lending definition and crispness. If the basic surfaces are in pretty good condition but lack zest, this type of detail can make a great difference.

Positioning is all-important. Natural breaks occur between the ceiling and wall, where a cornice would be; at picture-rail height; about a third up from the floor, where wainscotting would be; and at baseboard level.

Fresco

A toothed painted frieze and mottled paint effect are excellent ways of compensating for, respectively, the lack of a cornice and poorly finished walls (right).

Since only a relatively small surface area is involved, this type of detail can be bright and bold without running the risk of swamping the rest of the decoration. If the walls are quiet, a line of complementary color or black will sharpen up the effect. A frieze of stenciled motifs or sprayed-on stars can supply the type of interest normally supplied by plasterwork flourishes, while wainscotting patterned in paint will set up a lively opposition to an expanse of plain wall above. Painted-on baseboard moldings are a common feature of many European folk interiors. A rich terra cotta color taken about 8 inches (20cm) up the wall extends the tiled floors of rustic Italian villas visually and helps to disguise unsightly knocks and scrapes.

More fanciful ideas include festooning swags of objects united by a common theme and sprayed white to look like plaster; raiding suppliers of decorative detail for cherubs or other forms of sculptural relief; or sticking on stars and bosses to make bold punctuation points. Photocopiers come in useful for blowing up details to make pasted-down borders and friezes (see page 34). And you can print single motifs with almost anything – cut-up potatoes and sponges are excellent for making naive shapes of animals to march around nursery walls.

The antithesis of crisp architectural detail – such as freehand wiggly lines, dots, and chevrons – can be incredibly effective when used to trim and accentuate the top of a wall. On warm ocher, terra cotta or color washed walls, this type of uninhibited decoration has a distinctly tribal appeal.

FLOORS

Painted Floors

If your floorboards really need covering up but you can't afford carpeting or tiles, you can paint them instead. Floors coated with matt oil-based paints make ideal surfaces for stenciling a range of designs on. Widely spaced laurel wreaths give subtle decorative covering (far left). **Stylized flower shapes strike a rustic note** (left), **while random fish prints look lively underfoot** (right).

One new home owner, impecunious after buying her house, found that she could not stand the sight of the old carpet in the living room, with its luridly swirling, stomach-churning pattern. In a brilliant flash of inspiration, she turned the carpet over and discovered that the woven backing made a hard-wearing and perfectly acceptable base material for rugs, as unobtrusively elegant as sisal matting.

Not all flooring problems are so neatly solved, but there are a surprising number of cheap and cheerful ideas to improve matters underfoot. Simplicity is generally the best policy where floors are concerned, especially since most treatments are labor-intensive and time-consuming. Plain scrubbed boards with a scattering of cotton dhurries or rag rugs look infinitely better than cheap carpeting which will thin and age unattractively within the year. A more unusual version of this basic combination is to lay strips of rag runner along the main pathways through your rooms in a manner reminiscent of Scandinavian farmhouses.

Large sheets of plywood screwed in place make an appealing modern floor. Plywood can be very easily stained, stenciled, and varnished to increase decorative possibilities. In the same way, hardboard laid with the smooth side up and sealed with a couple of coats of clear or tinted varnish has the seamless sophistication of expensive linoleum floors.

When fine carpeting was even more costly than it is today and synthetic materials had not been invented, painted floorcloths were the economical alternative. The process of making a floorcloth is a little too laborious for the average amateur, but paint is still a good means of covering up poor floorboards or adding decorative flourishes in the form of stenciled borders and stylized motifs. You will need to use tough, oil-based paint on the floor if it is to wear well (yacht paints provide the best results). Although such finishes will take several days to dry, during which time the room will be out of use, the labor and expense involved are much less than those required to sand and seal old boards.

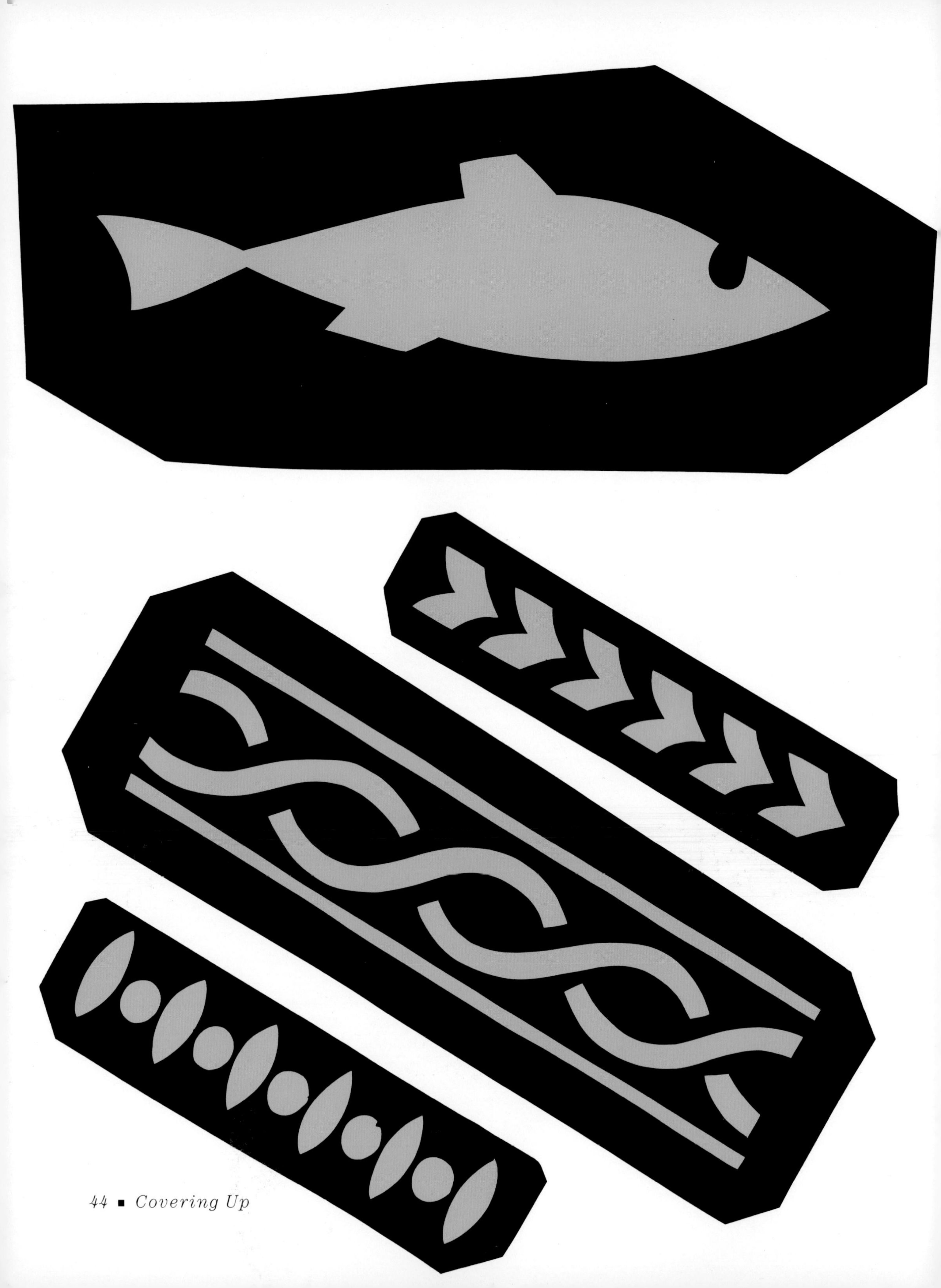

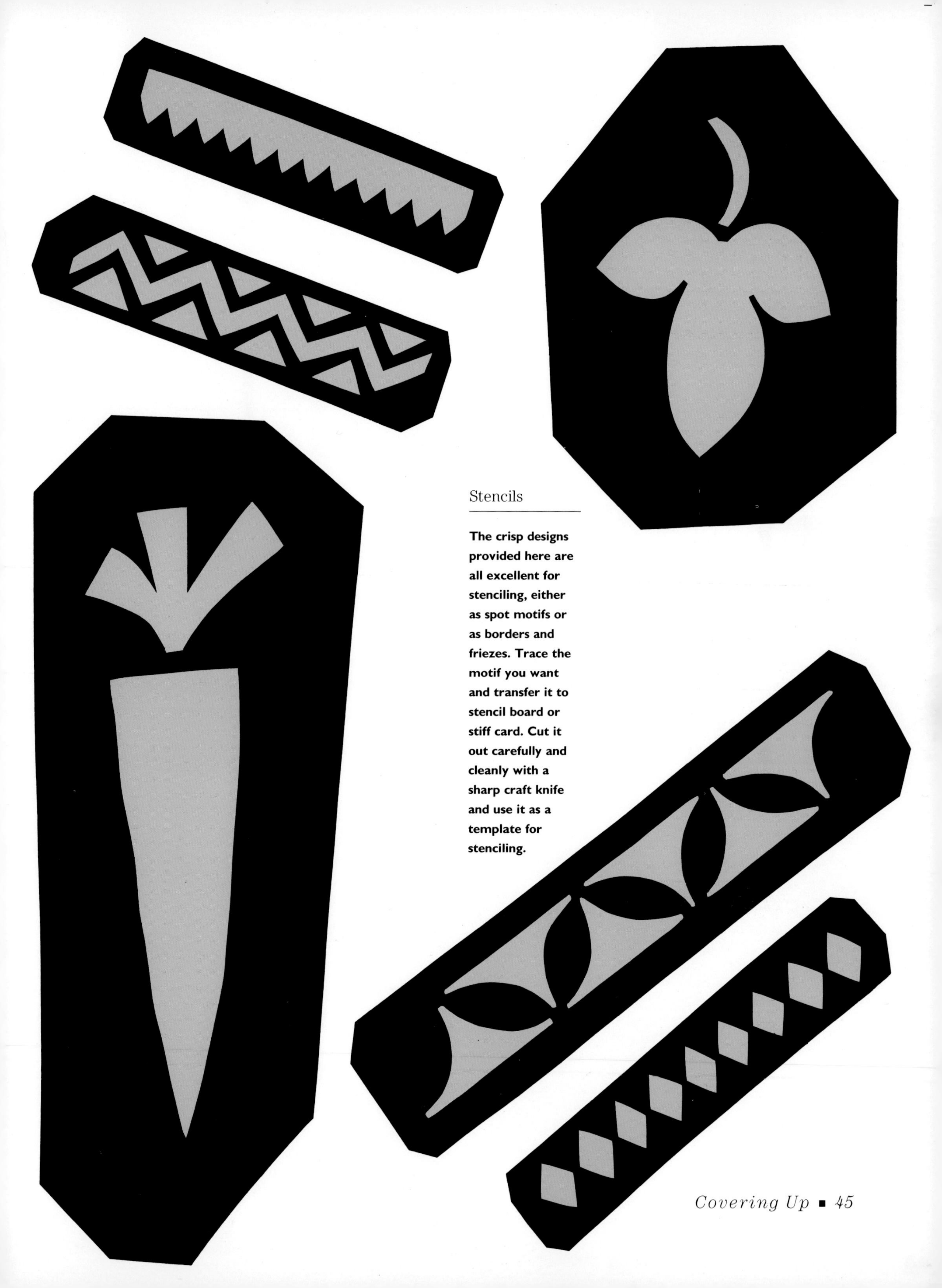

Stencils

The crisp designs provided here are all excellent for stenciling, either as spot motifs or as borders and friezes. Trace the motif you want and transfer it to stencil board or stiff card. Cut it out carefully and cleanly with a sharp craft knife and use it as a template for stenciling.

Window Dressing

WINDOW DRESSING

Many people are deterred from tackling window treatments by the received wisdom that the undertaking will devour their decorating budget. But despite their potential expense, they do offer great scope for originality and creative economy. And you don't have to be accomplished with a needle and thread to come up with dazzling effects that look every bit as impressive as the very height of soft-furnishing fashion.

Despite the relatively small surface areas involved, windows cannot be ignored. The focal point of any room, windows draw the eye, either by virtue of their architectural character or the view that they reveal. What is more, window treatments provide a natural opportunity to display color, pattern, and texture and to reflect the decorative style of the room, which is why so much effort and expense tend to be devoted to them.

In a very few cases, the whole issue can be sidestepped by doing without any covering at all. If the window is finely detailed, filled with beautiful stained glass, or if it is an unusually graceful shape (and if privacy and screening light are not important) the window can simply be displayed in all its glory. Most windows, however, demand some kind of dressing, if only for practical reasons. And few people are entirely comfortable at night in a room in which there are no curtains or blinds to draw against the dark.

Nothing suggests luxury more than soft folds of fabric falling to the ground in a graceful sweep, or billowing festoons floating over the top of the window frame. But don't despair if your budget does not stretch to elegant chintz with all the trimmings. The impression of luxury depends more on being generous with the amount of fabric than on the price per yard. The secret of creating sumptuous window treatments in an economical and effective way is to exploit the versatility of fabrics and materials not usually associated with soft furnishings.

FABRICS

If you are looking mainly for decorative impact, basic cottons such as muslin, calico, and cotton voile are a good starting point. Plain cotton is cheap, so you can indulge in yards of it. It is also light and easy to work with which makes it ideal for many quick-sewing or non-sewing techniques. And it can be printed, dyed, stenciled, and trimmed to your heart's content.

There is nothing new about using light, filmy drapery at windows. Many contemporary paintings of eighteenth-century interiors show muslin, lace, or light cotton either in conjunction with festoons or richer material or, as was often the case in summer months, as a substitute for them. In northern countries, where summer light was so welcome after the interminable gloom of winter, many windows featured the merest slip of lace, or muslin crowning the top of the frame, a little flourish in fabric rather than a full-scale covering. There is something inherently charming about the contrast between the ordered classicism of such rooms and their furnishings, and the light, fresh simplicity of the window dressing.

Light cottons are not the only option. The smooth, dense sateen-type of material normally used for lining can make stylish curtains in its own right, particularly as it is now available in a range of colors aside from the basic

Plain Sailing

This window fills almost the whole wall with little room at the sides or at the top from which to attach any covering. The neat solution uses lengths of cheap plain cotton simply tacked in place and drawn up in soft wings of fabric. Extra light control, essential in a bedroom, is provided by roller blinds (left)**.**

Window Dressing

neutral buffs and grays. Lining silk is also surprisingly affordable, although it may need to be weighted with a fringe or other trimming to make it hang properly. Striped, cotton mattress ticking is hard wearing, economical, fresh, and contemporary. Indian bedspreads patterned with "Tree of Life" or paisley designs would work well as curtains in a room with a Victorian or ethnic style of pattern. Felt is yet another possibility: it comes in a range of brilliant shades for warmth and depth of color. Sailcloth or unprinted artist's canvas both share a sculptural quality when hung in stiff folds, and are ideal for nautical-style blinds.

Antique curtains are no longer the bargain buy they once were, as those in good condition command relatively high prices. But junk shops and second hand stalls are still a good source of odd bolts of fabrics left over from the 1930s, '40s, and '50s, which would make an authentic and cheerful contribution to a retro-style room.

Don't neglect dress fabrics. Lengths of plaids, ginghams, stripes, and polka dots can sometimes be picked up on the remnant table and put to decorative use at the window. Fabrics blended with a percentage of manmade fiber often make good lightweight drapery, and the pattern ranges available are generally good. For a really theatrical effect, Indian saris are unbeatable. Simply drape them over the window, where the light shining through will intensify their iridescent color, their pattern, and glittering detail.

Light Touch

Filmy muslin has a long history of use as a window treatment, traditionally as lightweight undercurtains to filter bright sunshine. But this pretty semi-transparent fabric looks good enough on its own and is so economical you can afford to be generous with the amount (far left)**.**

Drapery

A bolt of glorious crimson glazed fabric, draped in deep swags over a pole and caught up to the left in an asymmetrical arrangement, adds to the Baroque splendor of this period room. When draping a window, it may take several attempts before you are satisfied with the way the fabric hangs (left)**.**

CURTAINS

At the simplest level, most materials can be draped over a pole or metal curtain rod to create something of the look of swags and tails. Lightweight cottons and semi-transparent fabrics can be knotted and swathed in all kinds of ways; heavier material may need a few retaining stitches or staples to keep the folds in place. The special virtue of these effects is that they are easy to dismantle, either for cleaning or if you just want to try something new.

If you would rather have curtains that can be drawn, there are several ways of making headings that involve minimal sewing. One basic method is to make a cased heading which gathers the fabric into soft folds as it is drawn along a pole or rod. To do this, simply fold down a hem at the top of each curtain and sew along the edge to create a channel of fabric, then thread the curtain onto the pole.

A variation on the same theme, which suits fabric with more body, is to cut into the casing to make scalloped or crenellated shapes. Alternatively, you can attach loops of tape at intervals along the top of the curtain, sew on brass rings, or eyelet the top of the curtain and thread ribbon or tape through to lace the fabric to the pole. To create a curtain with its own integral cornice, attach rings or tape to the back of the curtain some distance down from the leading edge and allow the top to flop over in soft folds. Make sure the heading is strong enough to support the weight of material. Incidentally, all these ideas can be adapted for doorways or beds. When calculating the amount of fabric, allow for hems at the top and bottom; curtains that draw need a fabric width of one and a half to two times the window width.

French Windows

Dress fabrics may not be as durable as conventional furnishing materials, but they provide a good source of color and pattern, often at a fraction of the cost. To make these sumptuous curtains for french windows, a bottle-green synthetic taffeta was chosen for its silky finish and iridescent color. The "curtains" are unheaded and attached to the curtain pole by means of sprung metal clips, which allow them to be gathered in folds. The "cornice" consists of another length of fabric draped over the pole; tasseled ropes make tie backs, and a small amount of material bunched in the hand into a "rose" and stapled in place provides the finishing touch.

Decorating and Trimming

Cotton is easy to dye; in fact, it was this quality that originally made it so popular as a furnishing fabric. Dip bright white muslin or new lace in tea for a soft, naturally aged tone, or dye plain cotton any shade under the sun to fit in with an existing decorative scheme. Muslin and other cottons also print well; the homespun look of the weave can be accentuated by naive block prints of animals, fish, shells, and other natural shapes. In a more sophisticated vein, classical designs such as stylized acanthus leaves stenciled in off-white onto snow-white muslin recreate the subtle textured look of fine damask. There are also excellent fabric paints available which enable you to paint freehand directly onto cloth.

You can further customize basic fabric with a whole range of trimmings – traditional and otherwise. Light muslin – widely used at the windows in early nineteenth-century Biedermeier rooms – was often graphically set off with black knotted or bobble-cotton fringing. Haberdashers as well as furnishing departments are a good source of ideas for livening up simple drapery.

Braid, bias binding, ribbon, and woven cotton tape can be sewn or glued on in rows across the hem of a curtain or blind, or right around the fabric to edge it in color. Bright yellow shapes appliquéd onto midnight-blue felt make a Matisse-style backdrop. If, as in this case, you use a light-colored fabric appliquéd onto a darker base fabric, cut away the base fabric from beneath the newly applied piece to maintain the bright contrast in color. For a shimmering, light-catching effect, you could sew or stick on sequins, small mirrors, or glass beads. Even sea shells can look great sewn onto muslin or toile (linen-cloth). Many shells already have small pinholes which make it easy to thread them.

Vibrant Color

A shocking pink scarf and its equally shocking yellow partner provide a jolt of color contrast to liven up a plain window. Plain muslin scarves are cheap and easy to dye bright colors, and you can trim the lower edge, as here, with glass beads for extra decorative quality and style (right).

Sari Splendor

For instant glamor and glitter, saris are hard to beat. Many of the more luxurious examples are encrusted with metallic embroidery, which catches the light for a sparkling effect. If the material is very light, you may need to weight the lower edge so that the drapery hangs flat (right).

Glittering Gold

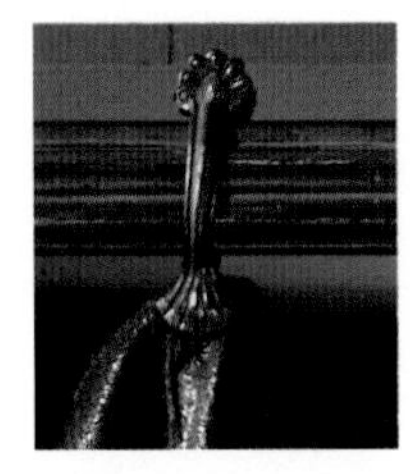

Starstruck

Make no-sew curtains with a dramatic star print using lengths of standard black interlining (the material used to make curtains light-proof). Measure the distance between the curtain rod and the floor and allow enough fabric for each curtain to rest in soft folds on the ground. Cut star shapes from folded paper (opposite) **in the pattern you desire and use the shape to cut a stencil template out of stiff card. Then spray the stars onto the matt side of the fabric using car spray paint. Gather up each curtain and attach at intervals using pinch clips available from upholstery outlets.**

Cornices and Accessories

Check Cornice

Cornices, fitted in place and covering a portion of the window, do not have to be elaborately constructed or tailored to be effective. Fabric can be fitted along the top edge to a batten and trimmed or cut along the lower edge for a dash of extra style (right).

Dotted Cornice

This deep cornice in dotted fabric is edged by a wide border in a bold animal-skin print. Iron-on interfacing or fabric stiffener attached to the back of the fabric allows it to be cut out to make a fancy decorative edge (right).

Most of the simplest drapery and curtain styles in this book will leave the curtain pole or rod in full view (conventional headed curtains are generally designed to be used with track which is hidden by a cornice). If your fabric and curtain style are inherently plain and unfussy, you can play up the element of contrast by going over the top with your accessories.

Wooden poles can be painted, stained, gilded, or varnished; they can be improvised using doweling and customized by sticking on wooden or metal finials. For an ultimately rustic look, suspend a branch of weathered driftwood from the windowframe to support a length of billowy muslin or a simple blind (see page 64–5). You could also dress up a basic metal rod with finials at either end, decorative brackets, cleats, and other paraphernalia for a look of instant Regency grandeur. Gilt and brass accessories can be very expensive – particularly antique ones – but you can salvage all kinds of interesting bits and pieces of ironware to achieve a similarly impressive effect.

Solid cornices that project over the top of the curtain to hide the heading and track are often nothing more elaborate than fabric-covered boxes. Stiff card or polyboard is easy to cut and shape, and can do the job just as well as wood panels: with fabric stretched over a layer of padding, stapled into place around a simple wooden frame and trimmed with braid, few people will notice the difference. Or you can experiment with building up layers of corrugated cardboard for a bold sculptural effect (see page 61).

Ropes and tasseled cords looped over hooks, bosses, or cleats make excellent tie backs for curtains (see page 68). For a softer, prettier look, tie a generous bow in a sash of contrasting or matching fabric.

CARDBOARD CORNICE

Boxed In

If your instant curtain or blind is stapled to the window frame, and you don't want to give the game away, you can hide the evidence with a cornice (left). **Corrugated card or packing material has a sculptural quality which is very appealing, and it is rigid enough to stretch across wide openings. Easily assembled, you need to construct a simple framework of battens to fit around the window frame – secure its joints with angle brackets and then nail into place. Cut the cornice shape you want – make sure you leave enough card at each end to wrap around the batten framework at the sides. Glue in place the main pieces and decorate the front with curls of lightweight cardboard** (right).

FRAMING THE VIEW

Cornice Frame

The basic cornice framework (right) **consists of lengths of 1×2in (25×50mm) stock cut to the required dimensions and joined at the corners with angle brackets. Angle brackets are also used to secure the cornice to the wall. For extra rigidity, you could add short lengths of wood at each corner to support the edges.**

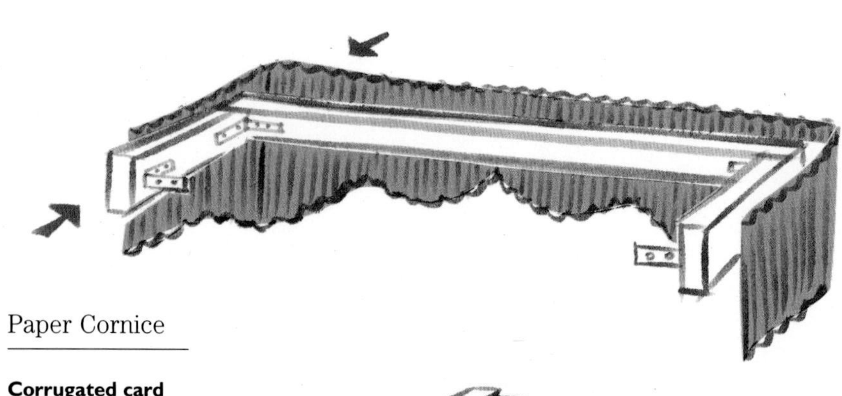

Paper Cornice

Corrugated card makes a stylish choice for instant cornices. Cut out the cornice to fit, and attach to the frame with glue. Decorate with cut swirls of card, or spray it gold (right)**.**

Over the Top

Use cardboard to imitate the extravagance of draped or carved cornices. Cut two mirror-image shapes and stick to the cornice frame with glue. Cover the central join with a shield shape and decorate it with paint (above and left)**.**

Fabric Covers

Basic card cornices make a good base for covering with fabric. Simply wrap the material around the card and glue down edges. To cover intricate shapes, cut notches into the fabric edge to allow a neat turnover. Stick bias binding, braid, or ribbon trim onto the fabric following the contours of the cornice for extra definition (above and right)**.**

Concertina

For a sculptural effect, fold card into narrow folds. You will need to join pieces of card with double-sided sticky tape to make a concertina long enough to enclose the frame; and leave two flat side pieces at either end where the cornice has to attach to the cornice frame.

Attach the concertina cornice to the frame by pinning or stapling into the folds (above and right)**.**

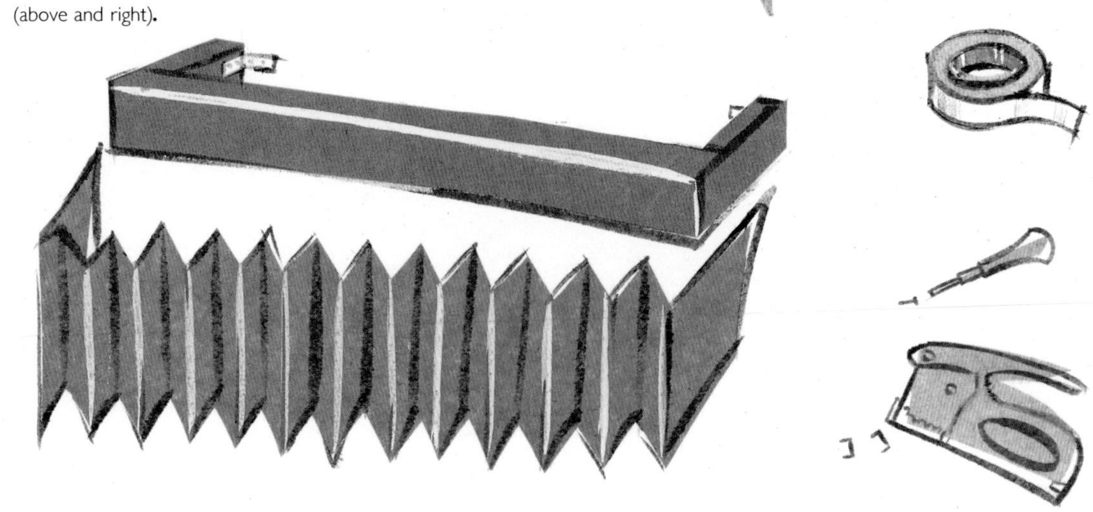

Driftwood

Natural inspiration was provided by this length of driftwood, utilized as a rustic curtain pole. Here, the driftwood is carefully balanced on long screws that have been driven partway into the wooden window frame; alternatively you could attach a pair of cuphooks or screweyes to the underside of the window recess and suspend the branch from those points. The hanging consists of eight squares of open-mesh dishcloths, stoutly tied and knotted together with short pieces of household twine.

No-sew Curtain

Nothing could be easier or more effective than this jaunty sweep of cotton thrown over a pole and gathered into a big knot at the level of the sill. Ensure that you buy enough fabric to extend right to the floor (left).

Tie Back

You can give the impression of luxuriously lined and finished drapery by tying a length of material in tight to make deep billowing folds. Here, rope wrapped neatly around a panel of hand-printed fabric makes a bold punctuation point (left).

RIBBONS AND BOWS

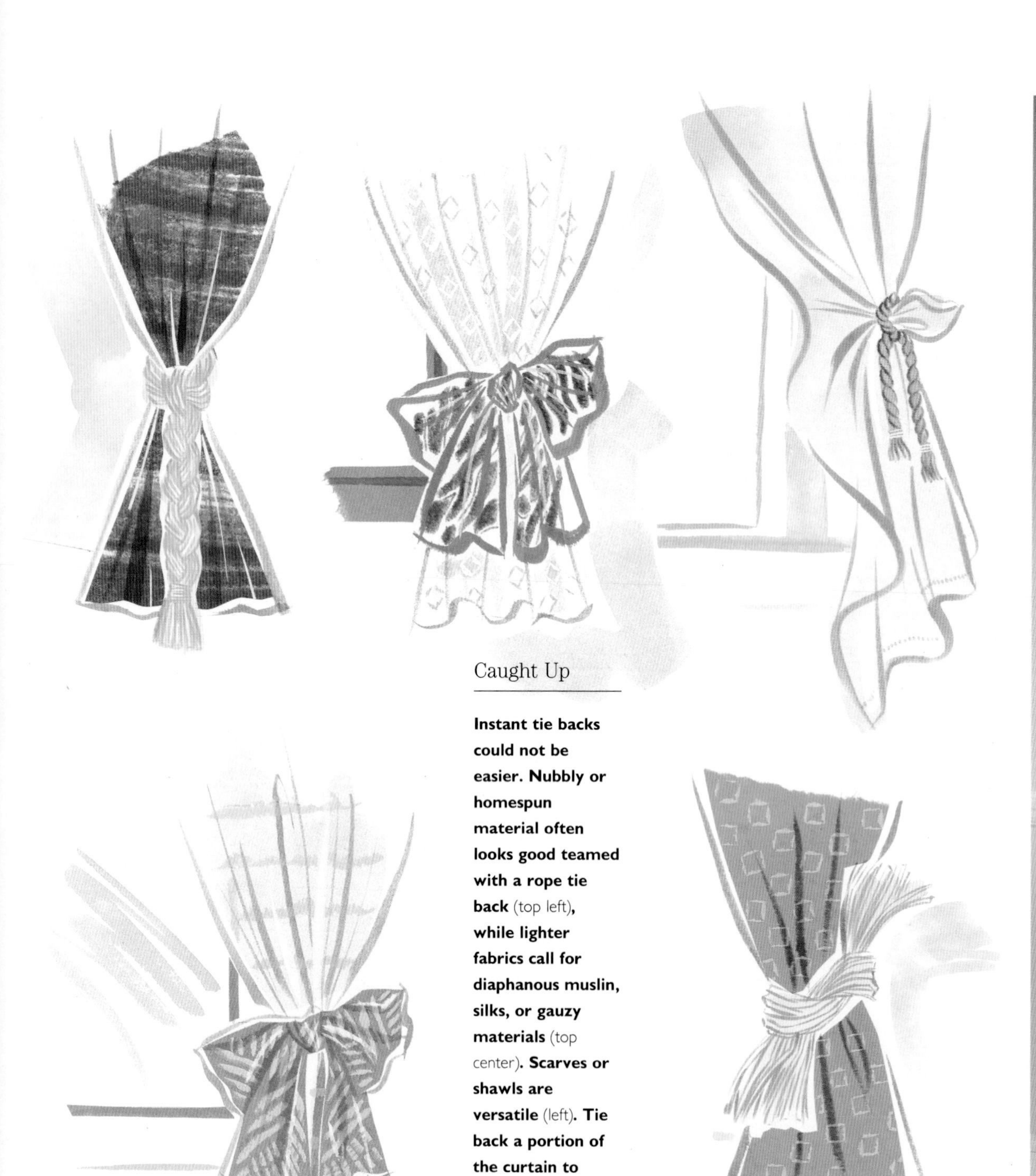

Caught Up

Instant tie backs could not be easier. Nubbly or homespun material often looks good teamed with a rope tie back (top left), **while lighter fabrics call for diaphanous muslin, silks, or gauzy materials** (top center). **Scarves or shawls are versatile** (left). **Tie back a portion of the curtain to leave rippling edges** (top right), **or experiment with maybe scrim or raffia** (right).

No-sew Cornice

A fabric cornice can be created with absolutely no sewing. Allow sufficient fabric to gather softly across the width of the window. Apply iron-on interfacing to the reverse of both top and bottom edges, turn over and press in place. Then cut vertical slits about 1½ inches (4cm) apart across the width of the cornice at the top and gather the fabric along a wide ribbon. The curtain itself is stapled or tacked directly to the window frame.

BLINDS

Awning

This improvised blind makes use of heavier-weight cotton in a broad stripe for the effect of an awning. Tacked in place along the top, long ties keep the neatly rolled lower edge in position. The crisp, striped design complements the checked sofa fabric and the cotton rug as well (left)**.**

Tied Blind

Blinds are ideal for kitchen windows, as they can be pulled up well out of the way. This simple treatment combines the practicality of a blind with the softness of a curtain. Long tapes hold the folds in place (left)**.**

Roller blinds in fabric, paper, and bamboo are cheap and easy to install. They can also be decorated and trimmed in much the same way as fabric drapery or curtains (see page 58). You can also improvise blinds using material that is too lightweight for conventional roller blinds by rigging up a system of pull-up cords, tape, or ribbon threaded through a pair of cup hooks. Alternatively, you can simply tie up the blind like a sail or awning and hold it in place using long tapes.

Although most people think in terms of fabric when it comes to covering windows, there are several other possibilities to consider which involve the use of different materials. If you do not need to worry about light control, but merely want to screen a view or gain a little privacy, you might consider filling the window recess with glass shelves to hold a collection of trailing plants, or lining up rows of colored glass bottles and containers to make a jewel-like display against the light. You could also stand a screen so that it blocks the view from the lower half of the window but allows light to spill through into the room at the top.

GATTI
TRA GENTE FELICE

Fast Furnishing

JUNK SHOPPING

Trimming

Most junk-shop finds need a little extra attention to bring them up to scratch. You can use upholstery trimming, such as this deep fringing, as a good way of disguising worn patches (left)**.**

Check It Out

Ordinary kitchen chairs look great painted in a bright positive color, and these flounced gingham skirts are easy to make. Attach iron-on interfacing to the top and bottom edges to make hems. Then cut vertical slits spaced about 1½ inches (4cm) apart and thread ribbon to gather the fabric up in pleats (far right)**.**

Makeshift furniture is not merely for those short of cash. Even in quite well-heeled households there is often room for simple pieces rigged up with basic materials. One example is the cheap, circular, particleboard table, disguised with a floor-length skirt of fabric held in place with a round glass top. These little dressed tables, holding a lamp and collection of well-chosen objects in the living room, or flanking the master bed, are something of a professional decorator's standby.

In the same spirit, you can make a kitchen dining table from a flush door and a pair of trestles. Cover the door with oilcloth and staple it in place. If you need to increase the size of an existing table, borrow a trick often used in restaurants and rest a large circle cut from particleboard or lumber core on top of the table, cover the board with felt, and add a floor-length cloth to hide the deception.

If the idea of improvised furniture conjures up a depressing image of mattresses on the floor, milk-crate tables, and scaffolding planks on bricks, think again. Such pitiful austerity is not the only alternative if the sofa of your dreams has a nightmare price tag or you'd need a second mortgage to buy a dining table and chairs. You can revamp old pieces with style, put a fresh face on tired tables and chairs, and jazz up junk without descending to the level of a student apartment.

There is no escaping the fact that good-quality furniture, antique or new, will always cost money, but putting some of the ideas in this chapter into practice will prevent you from falling into the common trap of rushing out to buy a poorly made approximation of what you really want. If you buy something you don't like just because it is what you can afford, you will have to live with it while you wait for it to fall to pieces (as it almost certainly will). And the chances are that this will happen before you can afford to replace it with what you wanted in the first place. It is far better to apply lateral thinking to the whole problem, brush up your decorating skills, use your imagination, and save up for the special sofa or bed.

JUNK SHOPPING

For basic tables and chairs, chests, and even the odd sofa or bed frame, junk shopping remains a good strategy. You are more likely to find solid, decently made pieces at prices you can afford in flea markets, secondhand stores, and salvage yards than in cut-price furniture outlets. It is also well worth putting up with a little wear and tear for the sake of character.

Junk shopping makes economic sense as long as you know where to go and what to look for. Forget any idea that you may discover a priceless hoard of antiques languishing in some dark corner of a dim, cobwebbed shop. The sophistication of the market, the proliferation of dealers and auction houses (some more scrupulous than others), and the eclectic nature of collecting today makes this an unlikely prospect. In the early part of this century, by contrast, the vogue was for furniture from the eighteenth and early nineteenth centuries. Victorian pieces, ignored and underrated, were therefore very well priced at that time. Nowadays, however, there is consistent demand for good pieces from all periods.

What does remain accessible is a plentiful supply of ordinary furniture (particularly from the 1930s onwards) that is practical, durable, and often with at least some period charm. Poor finishes – stained, worn, or discolored – can quickly and easily be covered up with a coat of paint. Shabby or stained upholstery can similarly be disguised under drapery if you can't afford recovering (see page 79). Look out for good, clean lines, intact, strong frames, and sound springs and seats on upholstered pieces. Avoid wooden pieces with telltale pinholes that indicate woodworm – they may easily infect your other furniture.

It is a good idea to prepare yourself for forays into the secondhand field by doing a little basic research on furniture types and styles, as well as acquainting yourself with good flea markets, stores, and auction houses specializing in the type of pieces you are looking for. Beware of impulse buying and take dealers' claims with a generous pinch of salt. If you are unsure about whether or not to buy, a small deposit will usually secure an item while you think it over.

Architectural salvage yards and dealers in reclaimed store fittings can also be a fruitful source. Old mahogany and glass store-display units, plan chests from designers' or architects' offices, and solid school cupboards are all good for storage. Trunks, wicker laundry baskets, and banks of drawers originally used for seeds, paints, or ironware are equally versatile.

Dedicated urban scavengers who make a habit of scouring dumpsters and building sites are constantly amazed at the quality of materials and furniture other people seem happy to discard. If you are eagle-eyed and skilled at minor repairs you may find the odd treasure poking out from under a pile of builders' rubble. (But if there is any doubt about whether the piece has really been thrown out, be sure to check with the owner before you haul it away!)

Wrapping Up

It's a Wrap

Plain muslin dyed in brilliantly clashing pink and yellow has been bound around a simple wooden chair, covering the frame and seat completely (below).

Dressed Chairs

Two different styles for the same chair have been created with black curtain interlining, used matt-side-out and sprayed with large gold stars. The legs of one are wrapped in scrim sprayed gold; on both, the fabric is stapled in place to give neat edges (left).

Many sofas and chairs with good, clean lines, strong frames, and a lot of life left in them are let down by shabby, stained coverings, which is not surprising as fabric wears out faster than wood. Unfortunately, loose covers elegantly tailored for a perfect fit or close-tacked upholstery with professionally piped seams demand the sort of skills which are not acquired overnight, and professional services tend to be expensive. While you are waiting for the check to come in, here are some solutions to tide you over.

Simplest of all is to drape the chair or sofa in a plain white cotton sheet (or you could dye the sheet in light, clear colors if you wanted). This tends to work best if more than one piece is draped – the look, of course, is the faded grandeur of out-of-season drawing rooms shrouded in dust covers. Draping is also a good strategy in minimal surroundings in which you are aiming for a crisp, modern look. These instant covers can unify a disparate collection of furniture at little expense and to dramatic effect. Again, as with window treatments, generous amounts of plain fabric suggests luxury; patterned or chintzy materials don't work in the same way. The special advantage of draping is that you can easily run the covers through the washing machine when they start to look grubby.

Using the same principle, plain cotton can be tied or wrapped around basic kitchen chairs to give them enough style for formal dining. For a rococo effect, finish them with a sweeping bow at the back.

If you would prefer to use patterned fabric for your soft furnishings, it is generally more effective to layer different materials in sympathetic colors and designs. A single Indian bedspread thrown over a sofa – no matter how beautiful the pattern – is more reminiscent of the crash pad than the bazaar. But using the same fabric as a base and adding fringed paisley shawls, woven throws, and cushions in complementary designs, you will achieve a rich patterning that is far from forlorn.

Loose Covers

Give a new lease of life to old armchairs by improvising loose coverings. Simple disguise can be very effective when orginal upholstery is worn or discolored (left). **You don't have to rely on white sheeting for instant cover-ups. More exotic and daring fabric choices lend an air of extravagance, such as this shimmering dress material** (overleaf)**, also seen draping french windows on page 52.**

DECORATIVE FINISHES

Sitting Pretty

Cheap pieces of furniture can be made more cheerful with exuberant patterns painted on them. There is no need for restraint – going over the top by applying vibrant color and design is much more effective than a half hearted or hesitant approach. Oil-based paints are more durable, but latex simplifies the job and produces excellent results. A chair and table base break out in a rash of dots (left)**, while rush-bottomed country chairs are enlivened with a freehand painted design** (right)**.**

The craze for stripping wood – particularly pine – has tended to obscure the potential of decorative furniture finishes. In the past, many pieces of everyday furniture were painted and enriched with patterns, often very colorfully. Such pieces were generally made of pine and other softwoods not considered fine enough to display in a more natural state. It was only furniture of higher quality, built in expensive mahogany, or veneered with exotic woods prized for the beauty of their figuring or their depth of color, on which the wood was shown off. The modern obsession with stripping has revealed wood that was always intended to be covered up.

For the instant decorator, there is good historical precedent for painting furniture. It is also quick and easy to do. Commercial stripping, carried out in bulk by dipping pieces into caustic baths, can damage fine detail. The alternative, which is to strip the piece yourself, takes hours of diligent application with glasspaper, solvents, and chemicals, taking off old layers of finish, filling cracks, and then refinishing with wax, varnish, or seal – a lot of work if the wood was never supposed to be given this kind of exposure.

For color and pattern inspiration, look at English cottage furniture, painted chalky blue or bottle green, or grained in attractive ochers and rich, smoky browns to give an impression of "woodiness." Then there are more exuberant examples in the folk-art idiom – the glowing reds and deep firgreens of Scandinavian furniture; the bold stenciled designs of Early Americana; the singing cobalts and turquoises of the Mediterranean; and the clashing limes, oranges and pinks of Mexican decor.

More refined than these robust rustic traditions are historical pieces from the eighteenth and early nineteeth centuries. The spare lines of Neoclassical furniture were often complemented by subtle, light coloring: washed Gustavian blues and grays; pale straw or ivory highlighted with black lining and gilding. Regency chairs and tables were decorated in delicate aqua-blue, gray-green, and gilt, or richly ebonized or lacquered in Chinese red.

Wooden furniture generally needs little in the way of preparation. A light sanding of gloss or varnished surfaces will ensure that fresh paint adheres properly. You can fill cracks and holes if you like, although this isn't necessary if you are aiming for a rustic look. Traditionalists recommend painting wood with oil-based paint, and for a single-color treatment with a smooth finish, this is probably the best choice. Eggshell is subtler and less obvious than high-sheen gloss, which can look tacky and over-shiny. But water-based latex is the surprising choice of many contemporary furniture painters. Quick-drying and easy to use, latex covers well and provides a good surface for subsequent decoration, with the final finish much closer to the matt look of old painted pieces.

Painting not only freshens worn or discolored finishes, but can serve to unify a disparate collection of country chairs or give an undistinguished table a jolt of style. Emphasize good lines by painting simple side tables black for Hoffmann-style modernity, or decorate a set of children's chairs in different paintbox colors. You could also paint cupboards and chests to match the wall color, increasing the sense of space in a room by simplifying the decoration and

making the furniture blend in with the walls. An "unfitted" kitchen composed of Welsh dressers, cupboards, and other free-standing pieces might benefit from this approach.

As with basic wall decoration, aged or distressed finishes can be more sympathetic and easier on the eye than glistening fresh paint. At its simplest, painted wooden furniture can be distressed merely by sanding back the paintwork along the edges and corners, where one would expect the finish to have worn. More elaborately, there are various recipes for crazed or crackled finishes if a more overt look of age is desired. You can also experiment with layers of different washes or glazes to build up the richness and depth of color associated with the mellowing effects of time (see pages 26 and 27). Instant "gilding" can simply be drawn in using metallic felt-tipped pens.

These distressed effects work well with other forms of painted decoration for a robust, farmhouse look. Stenciled or freehand painted patterns can liven up drawer fronts, chair backs, bedheads, and cupboard doors. Traditional motifs include flowers, garlands, hearts, stars, and naive birds and animals. You can also add dates and initials.

Set off large motifs on panels and other flat surfaces with simpler borders on the legs or outlining the frames of a piece of furniture. Leaf shapes, spots, chevrons, and rococo swirls emphasize the lines and generally add to the decorative exuberance. Don't be fainthearted: less is not more when it comes to recreating traditions of folk decoration. Bright, dashing colors and layers of vibrant pattern express the powerful creative energies of these charming country styles.

Vinegar Graining

The traditional method of graining wood used a recipe containing stale beer. This modern update substitutes vinegar. First paint the surface with a coat of flat matt latex in a light color: yellow works well grained with brown; for richer effects, try brick-red or gray-green grained in deeper tones of the same color. Leave the paint to dry. Then make the graining glaze. Mix two tablespoons of vinegar with half a teaspoon of sugar and add powdered color (brown, black, dark red, or dark green) until the glaze runs freely. Brush onto the surface and then distress with a rolled-out piece of putty or a similar material, wiping off excess paint from time to time onto paper towels. Try out different directions to vary the pattern.

TOP TABLES

Patchwork Top

A junk table painted in a solid color has a patchwork paper top assembled from torn scraps stuck down with wallpaper paste. When the paste has dried, seal the table top with a coat of clear matt varnish (below)**.**

Instant Regency

Gold lines are drawn on a matt-black latexed surface with a felt pen to lend this simple table a sophisticated look. A whole star anise sprayed gold is a surprising substitute for a bronze mount (right)**.**

Mosaic

A mosaic border encrusts a table top. Apply a layer of grout, thick enough to inset the mosaic, and color the grout with a coat of latex. Press each piece in firmly and allow the grout to dry overnight (right)**.**

SITTING PRETTY

Tartan Chairs

Sit down in style on bold tartan chairs. Paint a base latex coat and leave to dry. Then build up a plaid effect in cross-hatched stripes, using sweeping confident brushstrokes. Don't worry if the stripes are not perfectly even – imperfections are a part of the charm (left)**.**

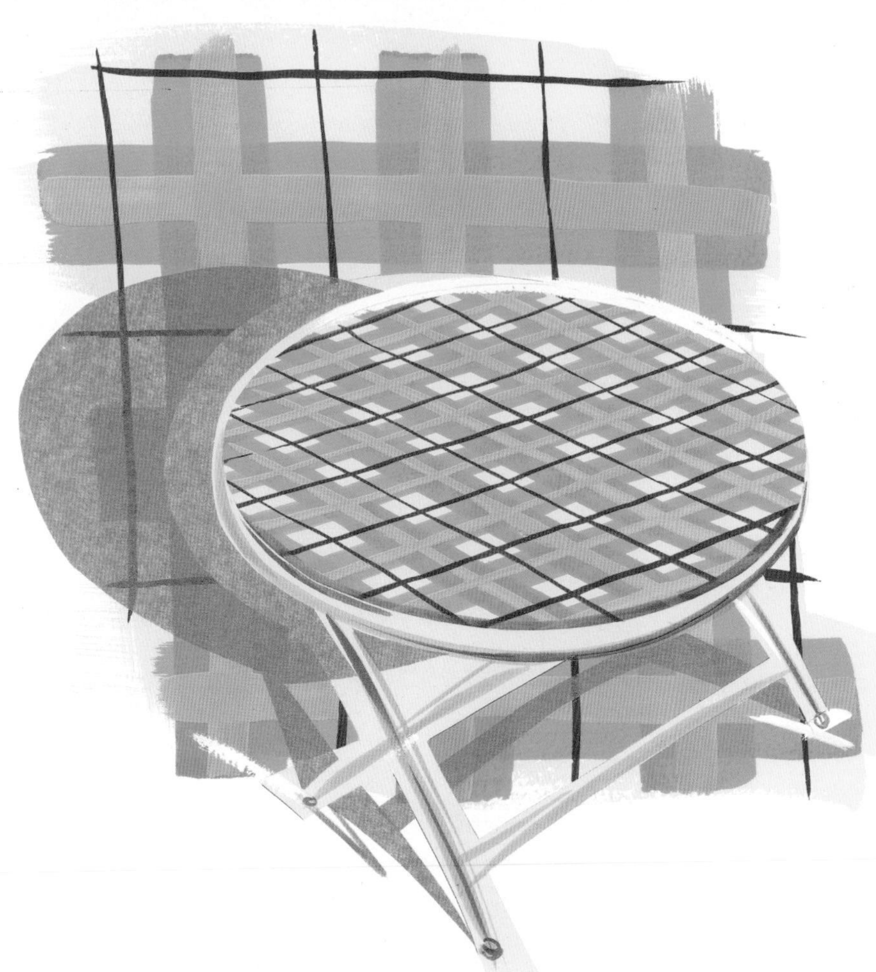

Checked Table

Apply a coat of matt black latex to legs and base and cover the top with a coat of matt white. The checked finish is determined by the brush width. Use a square-ended, soft-bristled watercolor brush. Mix white and black for a soft mid-gray, and thin with water for transparency. Paint gray stripes over the white base in one direction, then cross-hatch in thinned black paint. Wait for each coat to dry before going on to the next (above)**.**

New From Old

An alternative to painted decoration is *découpage*. Despite the rather grand name, this technique involves nothing more elaborate than cutting out paper pictures and gluing them in place onto a wall or a piece of furniture. Wrapping paper and greeting cards can be good sources of images to stick on a chair back or cupboard front. A coat of varnish will protect the paper cut-outs. *Découpage*, a favored pastime of leisured Victorian ladies, often works best in a rather quaint idiom, featuring posies of flowers, cherubic children, and garlands. You could also adapt the same technique and collage postcards or labels onto a table top for a more up-to-date look.

Still in the stick-on department, you can create patterns and borders three-dimensionally with a variety of customizing materials. Brass or metal upholstery tacks can be used to edge drawer fronts or worked in repeating geometric designs, and are very effective on chests of drawers or trunk lids. Plain wooden molding can be stuck onto cupboard and closet doors to give the look of solid paneling in an instant. Even braid, gimp, and ribbon can be stuck on as drawer or table edgings for a decorative "lift."

Metal furniture offers its own decorative possibilities. The wonderfully evocative verdigris of old metal – the weathered, green-rust finish of park chairs and café tables exposed to the elements – is the height of current decorative fashion. But if real decay does not appeal, there are a number of excellent one-coat metal paints that will cover rusty surfaces with little or no preparation. These are generally available in metallic or flat colors and in textured or silky smooth finishes.

Collage Screen

Simple screens are not hard to make using precut standard panels of board secured with screen hinges. The fun begins with decoration: cover with fabric or felt stapled in place and trimmed with glued-on braid or ribbon; spatter with flecks of paint or stripe with a cut roller; or collage, as here, with a vivid patchwork of patterned paper which is sealed with a coat of clear matt varnish to protect the surface (left)**.**

Screen Test

Tartan Screen

Decorate a screen using cut-and-tied rollers to create a plaid paint effect (see page 24). The roller, instead of being cut into broad bands, was cut and tied into finer sections. A final coat of blue-tinted varnish softened the tones of paint (left)**.**

Leaf Screen

This leaf screen features photocopied prints of an acanthus leaf. Two panels of the screen are covered in full A3 sheets, butted up. When stuck lengthways with wallpaper paste these exactly fill the width of our panel. The other two panels feature greater enlargements of the leaf for a more abstract effect. The screen was protected with acrylic varnish tinted with veridian green watercolor paint (right)**.**

Hiding Away

Kitchen Tidy

Sunny checked washable fabric gathered on plastic-coated wire hides kitchen clutter from view, but allows easy access to shelves. A matching tablecloth helps to give coherence to a busy room (left).

Storage Units

Save old boxes, baskets, and containers of every description to help ease storage problems in children's rooms and work areas. Shoe boxes can be given a new life covered in wrapping paper, and baskets can be painted to blend in or left plain (right).

Accessible, workable storage is essential to the running of any household, and it also keeps the emphasis where it belongs. If you want the elements of a room to work harmoniously and for displays to be effective, you need to eliminate clutter.

There never seems to be enough space for storage, even in the best-run households. Building in closets and cupboards is expensive, and only worthwhile if you intend to stay in your home for a considerable time. It is often better and certainly cheaper, therefore, to exploit the versatility of containers to take the overflow.

Trunks, blanket boxes, and covered laundry baskets can hold a myriad of household items including toys, shoes, linen, or magazines. Vegetable racks made of plastic-covered wire can be used for storing bathroom accessories, towels, stationery, or diapers and changing equipment. Many home improvement stores stock inexpensive sets of drawers in clear plastic or unfinished wood, for storing nails, screws, and other hardware; you can put these to new uses storing spices, jewelry, or cosmetics. In addition, a good supply of baskets is useful in children's rooms, kitchens, and bathrooms.

Painted garden trugs, orange boxes, or fruit crates from the supermarket make virtually free storage boxes. Cheapest of all, cardboard hat- or shoeboxes dressed up with wrapping paper or fabric and neatly labeled provide an instant organization system for filing letters, bills, receipts, and photographs. There's nothing new in this practice – bandboxes covered with leftover scraps of wallpaper provided a means of instant storage originally used in the nineteenth-century.

Hanging Space

Clothes left out hanging on a rail get dusty and fade in the sunlight; built-in closets are expensive and armoires and hutches are bulky. If you have an alcove to spare, beside a chimney for instance, this curtained hanging space provides a stylish solution, as well as protection for your clothes. Measure the width of the alcove and buy two expanding sprung metal rods of the correct length. Fit one inside the alcove as a clothes rail. Fit the second at the top, outside edge of the recess. Then hang doubled lengths of plain muslin over the higher rod – as many as you need for the desired effect – and tie in front with raffia, scrim, or ribbon. Alternatively, you can make rods from lengths of 2 inches (5cm) diameter wooden dowels slotted into metal fittings.

BEDS

The bed was once the single most important piece of furniture in a household, handed down from generation to generation; in grand houses they were the focus of lavish expenditure on costly hangings and trimmings. Beds no longer hold such special significance but still have a vital role to play in our well-being and comfort.

When it comes to buying a mattress it is important never to cut corners. Cheap mattresses are a classic example of a false economy, and can harm your posture and lower your vitality. However, there are plenty of shortcut ways to trimming and furnishing a bed.

Enclosing a bed or bed alcove with fabric gives a suggestion of the grand beds of the past. Many of the ideas and fabrics suggested for the window drapery section, would work equally well as instant bed hangings, although you will need a framework from which to hang the drapery. A fine metal rod projecting out from the wall could take a sweep of light fabric to either side of a bed or you could attempt a basic wooden framework to decorate or drape as an instant four-poster.

Dressed Beds

Fabric canopies and hangings are wonderfully evocative and romantic, and make a refreshing alternative to thick bed curtains. Billowing clouds of muslin have been dyed palest blue and looped over a simple frame, tinging the early morning light (left)**. A filmy Indian sari with woven borders makes a serene canopy, draped over a frame of metal poles** (far left)**.**

Bed Hangings

Canopy Bed

Drape a bed hanging overhead to create the effect of a canopy. Support a pole on two hooks screwed into the wall. Hang another pole from short lengths of rope or tape looped over another pair of hooks screwed into the ceiling at the bottom end of the bed (right)**.**

Arabian Nights

A variation on the same theme, this delicate sari fabric is draped over poles held in place by pairs of metal pole holders attached to the wall behind the bed and to the ceiling (left)**.**

Tester Bed

A picture frame is the basis for this grand effect (left)**. Suspend the frame to the ceiling on short lengths of chain hung from stout hooks. Make sure that the hooks are screwed into the ceiling joists, not just into the plaster; check the position of joists by lifting floorboards in the attic or room above, or drill fine test holes in the ceiling. Staple a fabric cornice and bed curtains to the inside of the frame.**

Four-poster

Lengths of bamboo or garden cane make a lightweight framework for filmy muslin or net drapery. Lash the canes together with stout twine or cord and suspend from the ceiling using butcher's hooks threaded through screw-eyes (right)**.**

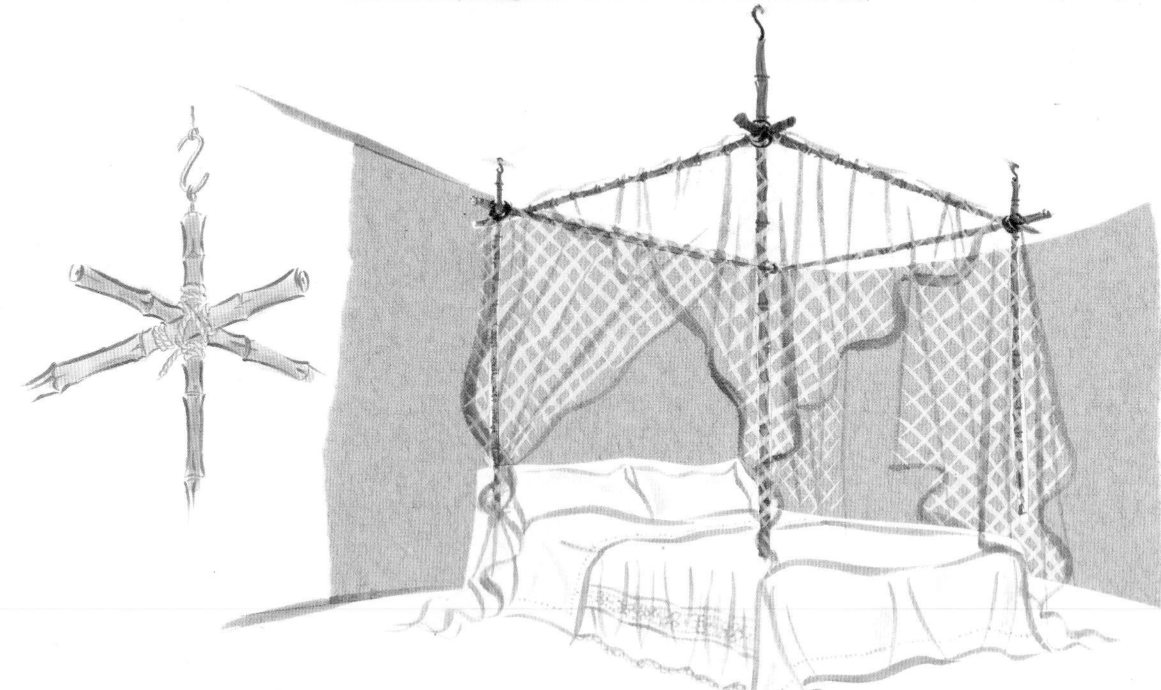

Sweet Dreams

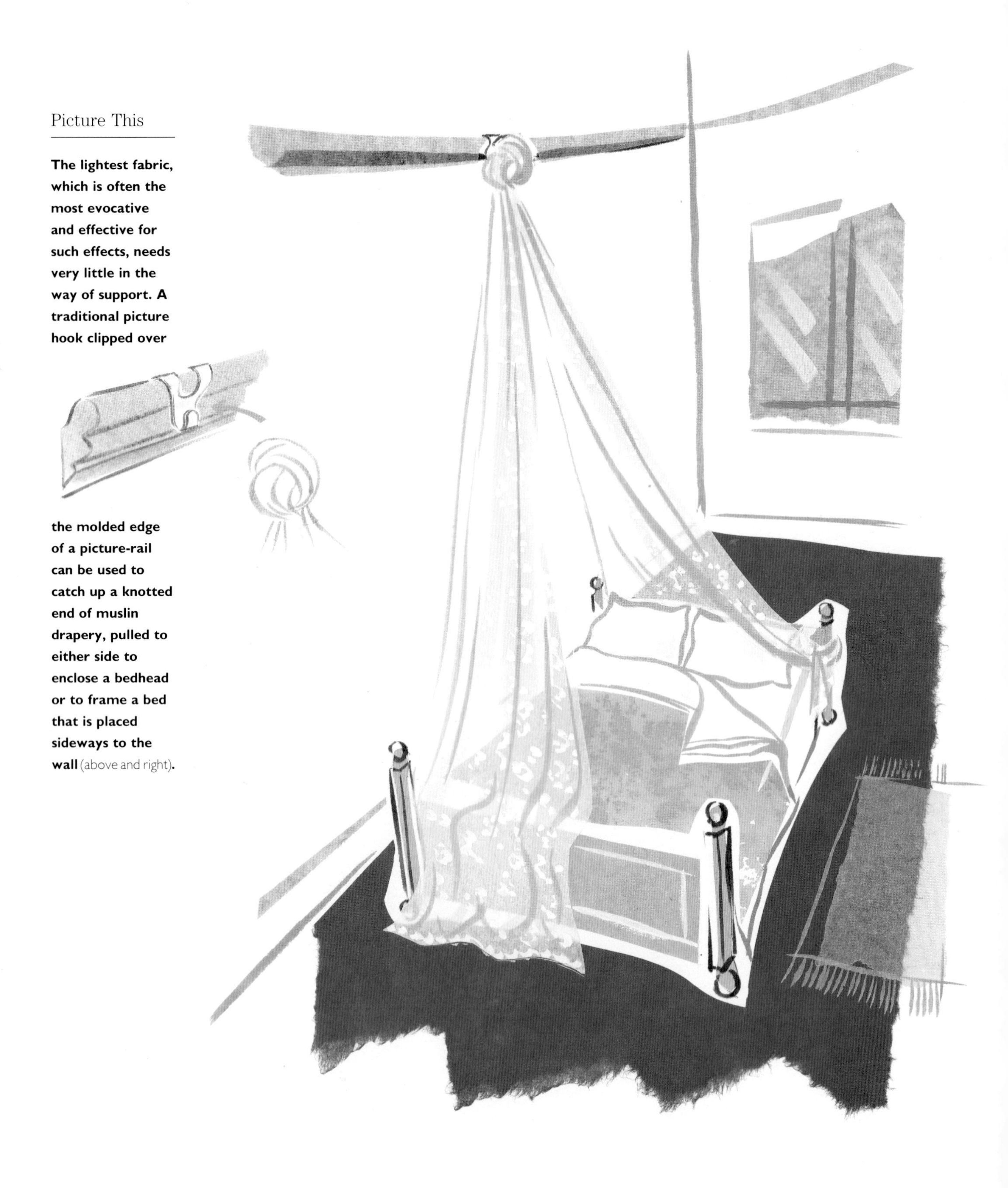

Picture This

The lightest fabric, which is often the most evocative and effective for such effects, needs very little in the way of support. A traditional picture hook clipped over the molded edge of a picture-rail can be used to catch up a knotted end of muslin drapery, pulled to either side to enclose a bedhead or to frame a bed that is placed sideways to the wall (above and right).

Mosquito Net

Borrow an idea from the tropics and screen the bed in fine netting. Wrap a metal hoop in net, sewing fabric tapes inside to keep the hoop in position. Then pull the top taut and knot in place. The netting can be drawn back and tied at either side (right).

Instant Bedhead

Pinch or sprung clips, usually available from upholsterers', are decorative in their own right and strong enough to support pillows or cushions on a pole for an instant bedhead (left).

SHOWING OFF

Showing Off

The something-for-nothing approach to decorating really comes into its own when the issue is display. Pictures, treasures, mementoes our lives would be immeasurably poorer if we were denied the opportunity to show off the things we enjoy and value. Displays are intriguing because they reveal individual tastes and interests; more than any other aspect of decoration, they lend warmth and personality. And because they can be changed frequently and readily, they are one of the best ways of creating a new look.

Showing off is not a question of displaying status. There is something deadening about a collection of perfect porcelain acquired for investment potential; what counts is not the value of the objects on show, but what they

More is More

The sheer density of collections is the secret of their appeal. A montage of precious family snapshots chronicles the years (above)**. Tin toys have a lasting attraction for the young at heart** (right)**. A tartan army of plates, cups, and bowls multiplies the decorative impact of a basic design idea** (far right)**.**

mean to you. Wit and humor can be particularly engaging, transforming the everyday by making you look at it afresh. Hats hung on the wall like trophies, kitchen paraphernalia in sculptural arrays, or garish tin toys on the mantelpiece conjure visual magic out of the ordinary.

Even if what you put on view is no more functional than a piece of driftwood or a pile of beach stones, showing off can have its strategic uses. Clever arrangements draw the eye, directing the attention away from less-than-perfect baseboard moldings, pockmarked walls, and other imperfections. By inviting you to relish color, texture, or sheer eccentricity, this kind of decorative exuberance can help to make up for shortfalls in other areas.

AUSTRALIA

Rules of Display

Successful displays are all about creating impact. Scale, theme, positioning, and lighting are aspects to consider, whatever you display.

Scale is one of the most important issues – and often the most neglected. A collection of small jugs dispersed around a room on various table tops, for example, contributes little decorative interest. The same collection, brought together in one place, "reads" as a whole, immediately increasing the impact and attracting attention. Almost all collections owe a great deal of their appeal to the fact of being grouped, and it is this feature which deserves to be emphasized. By collecting objects or pictures in a group, you increase the scale of the display and prevent the fragmented look which results when things are just scattered randomly around the room.

When you collect objects together, you reveal their common denominator. You can have fun making up groups based around themes which appeal to you. Color is an obvious link. Groups of similar objects in the same color can be very powerful: rows of green plates on a Welsh dresser; blue glass jars on a window sill; or white shells on a bathroom ledge. Equally, the theme of a collection could be type, material, texture, or origin. Victorian amateur naturalists prized their specimen cases of birds' eggs and butterfly wings; and today many people are intrigued by the graphic virtuosity of labels, packaging, matchboxes, and other emphemera of consumerism. Remember that the point is not to aim for a collection of identical objects, but to create interest through diversity. Subtle variations on the theme – even the occasional jarring contrast – will bring it all to life.

There are many natural locations for display. The mantelpiece lends itself to balanced symmetrical arrangements, while large objects can be grouped on the floor to one side of the hearth if the fireplace is not in use. Deep sills and window ledges are ideal for displaying glass or other materials which gain sparkle and intensity with light shining through them. Alcoves and corners can be fitted with shelves, and a deep rack or shelf at picture-rail height can be used to display a collection of plates, platters, dishes, or jugs.

You don't have to be a museum or gallery curator to appreciate the importance of display lighting. All displays are enhanced by good lighting, natural as well as artificial. A table lamp will emphasize a tabletop collection; candlelight can add drama to a mantelpiece display. Mirror is an invaluable aid to spreading light, with objects ranged in front of it gaining the benefit mirror lends. Directional lighting can be angled to highlight a Welsh dresser packed with crockery, and a pendant lamp hung low over a dining table will make a pool of light over a centerpiece arrangement.

Shell Detail

Concave shells, such as these scallops attached to a mantelpiece, can also be used to adorn walls or chimneys by filling the backs with quick-drying filler and then gluing them in place. Both the starfish and scallops shown here have been sprayed with gold paint and then slightly dulled with shoe polish (left).

Grained Shelf

A simple shelf cut from man-made board has been given decorative lift: painted reddy brown and then mottled using black vinegar graining (see page 83), it forms the basis for a simple assembly of natural textures (below).

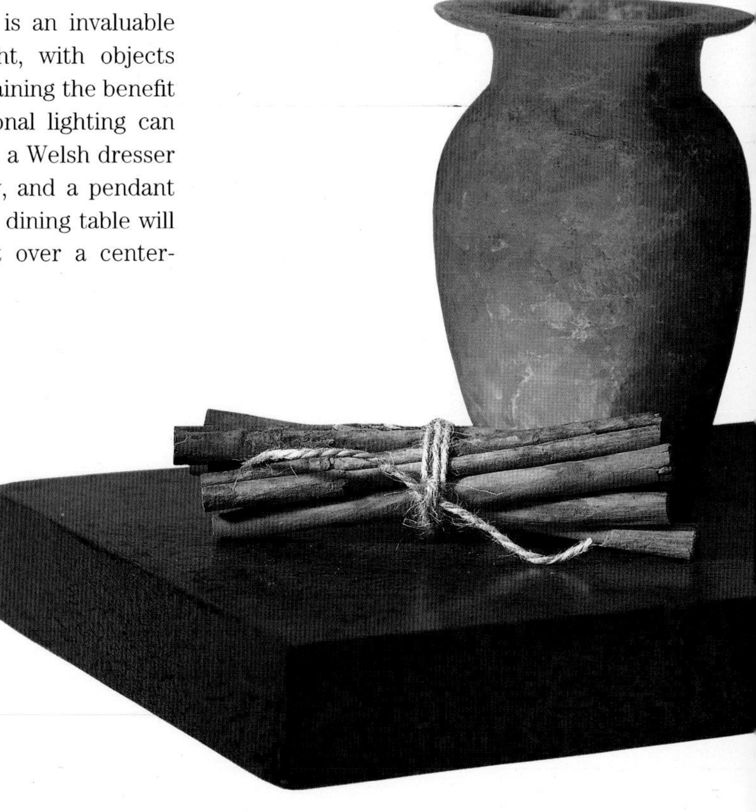

PRACTICAL PLEASURES

Everyday display makes a virtue of necessity, combining beauty with practicality. This is the charm of the *batterie de cuisine*, the hallstand, or the Shaker pegboard, where storage and display are combined.

The kitchen is an obvious location where usefulness is compatible with decorative interest. Kitchen utensils have a special sculptural appeal hanging from hooks over a counter. A row of gleaming pots and pans is equally effective and instantly accessible on display, organized but good looking too. Jugs bristling with wooden spoons, open shelves of brightly labeled tins, and jars and bowls of fresh fruit and vegetables can form displays that marry efficiency with visual pleasure.

The appeal of the Shaker ethos rests on just this celebration of practical, well-made things. Shaker-style pegboards were originally used to suspend everything from chairs to brooms: what was not in active use was hung up out of the way in a simple yet systematic orderliness. For the like minded, similar pegboards or rows of hooks can be adapted for displaying and tidying toys, clothes and bathroom accessories.

Bookshelves are another example of display storage. Books furnish a room, according to the saying; they convey warmth, liveliness, and character. At the same time they are demanding in terms of space. Bookcases and shelving at the cheaper end of the market can be particularly unappealing, lacking all style and distinction, but a few simple tricks can make the shelves look like they are part of the room rather than an afterthought. Wooden shelves, especially those built into alcoves, often look better painted the same color as the main wall. You can glue a strip of molding along the leading edge of each shelf to give the appearance of greater depth and solidity. Upholstery tacks, fringing, or the type of scalloped or toothed edging traditionally known as dust frills are other ways of dressing up plain shelves. Alternatively, you could wrap each shelf in fabric or felt, glued or stapled in place (see page 112). This type of upholstered look works particularly well for shelves within display cupboards.

Open Shelves

Ordinary, every-day household objects don't need to be hidden away. Open shelves, especially in kitchens and eating areas, look both warm and hospitable. A rough hewn Welsh dresser is trimmed with dried country branches (far left)**. Half-round sections cut from stout twigs and glued in place make corrugated edging for plain shelves** (left)**.**

Kitchen Ceramics

A collection of slipware provides color and pattern inspiration for the free hand decorative paint borders on this shelving unit built into a kitchen alcove (left)**.**

CUPBOARD LOVE

Lining

The interiors of cupboards and kitchen armoires in constant use are seen as frequently as their exteriors. Make the view special by lining plain backs and shelves with fabric to complement the objects contained inside. Fold over the edges to prevent fraying, and stick in place using fabric glue (left)**. A revamped wall cupboard acts as a means of display area for shells and other seaside treasures** (above)**.**

SHELVE IT

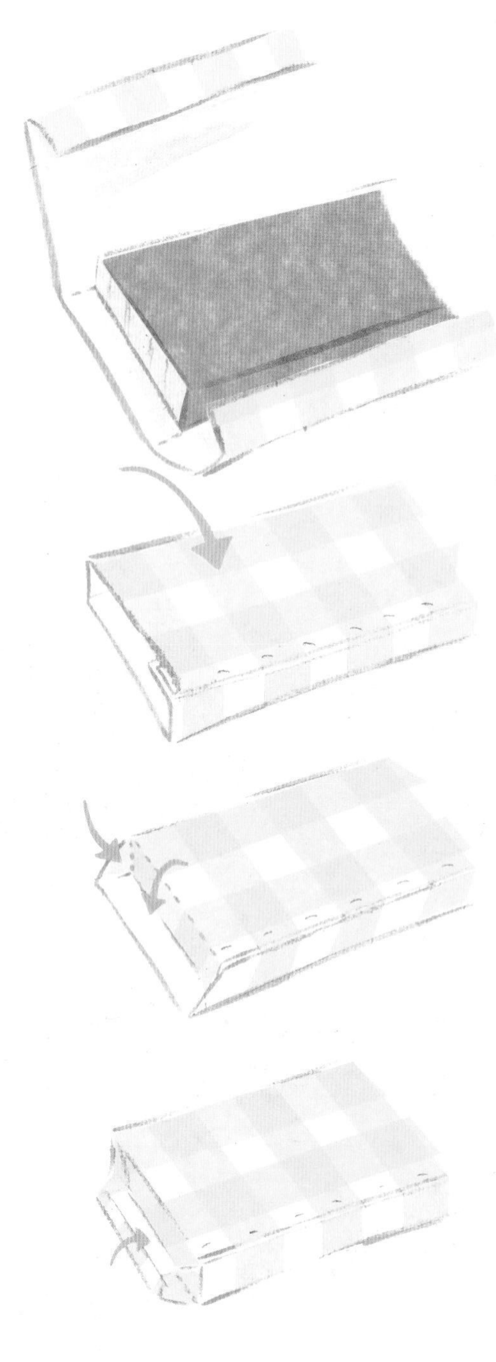

Wrapped Shelves

To completely enclose a shelf, turn up the back edge first and secure with glue, then bring the fabric around and fold over the top edge for a neat join. Secure with glue, pins, or staples. Fold and miter the corners just as if you were wrapping a gift (left)**. Alternatively, if the base of the shelf will not be on view you can leave the underside uncovered, as shown** (right)**. Shelves *in situ* can be wrapped by attaching fabric first underneath at the back edge and then bringing the fabric around, and folding over the top edge for a neat, clean finish** (below right)**.**

Lined Up

Wrapping adds instant style to uninspiring shelves and old storage boxes. Stripes, checks, and other geometric prints lend a note of tailored distinction, complementing the rectilinear lines of shelving, but you will have to exercise some care to make sure all the edges and corners line up correctly (right)**.**

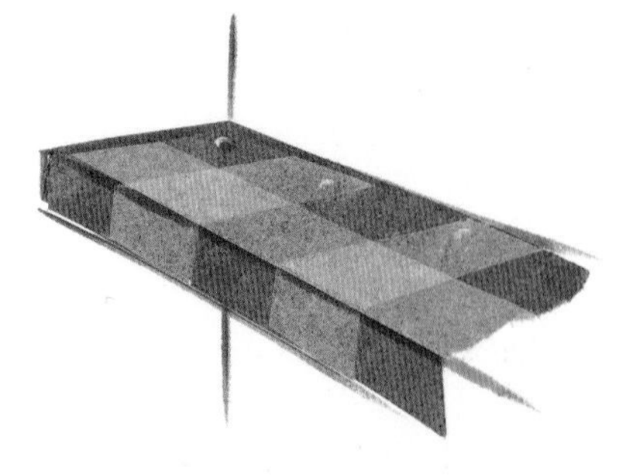

Nature's Way

Display Boxes

Small wooden drawers, printer's trays, and cardboard boxes make ideal compartments for display. Place or glue treasures inside and hang the unit on the wall using either a ribbon or cord (above and right).

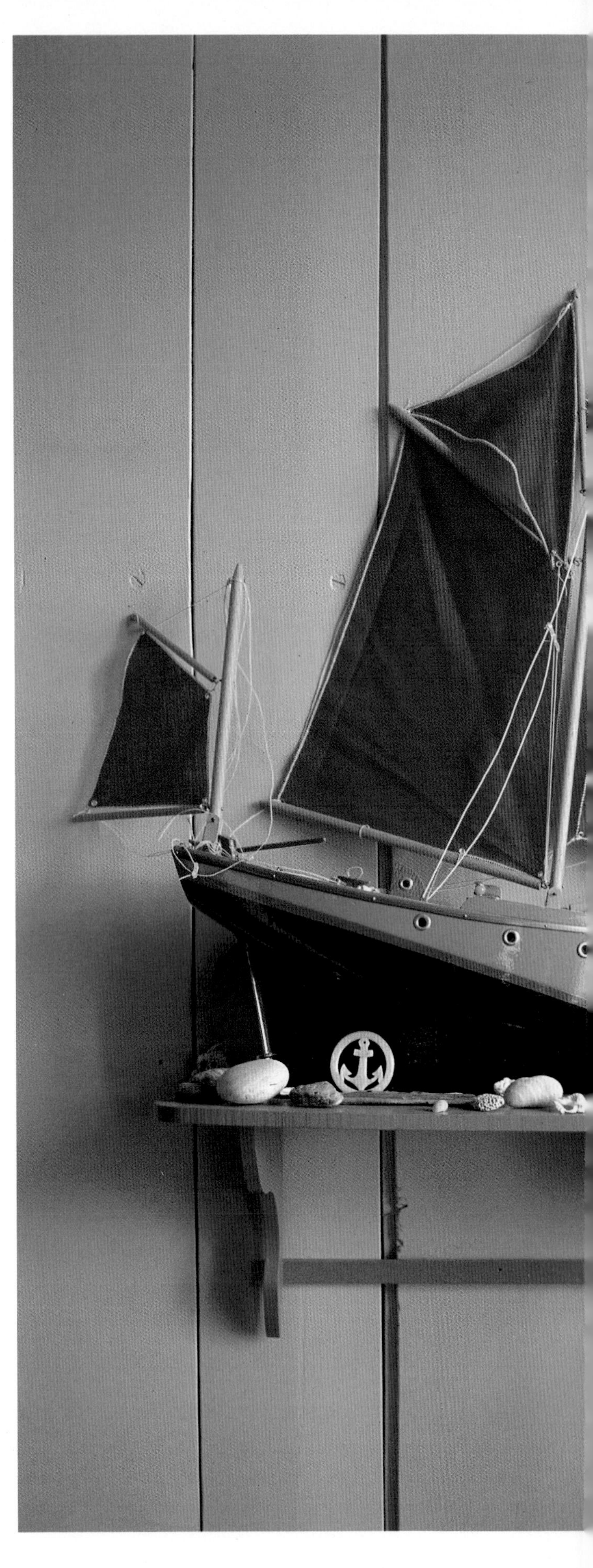

Themes

A hanging shelf carries a cargo of beach pebbles and a model yacht for an ocean-going theme (left). **Salvaged wood, worn by wind and water, is stuck straight onto the wall to frame fallen leaves** (right).

Cubbyholes

Wooden cubby-holes wrapped in newspaper make a textured display box. The open back is covered with scrim. Thinned water-based acrylic varnish, tinted a mahogany color, is patchily absorbed by the paper (above).

PICTURES AND FRAMES

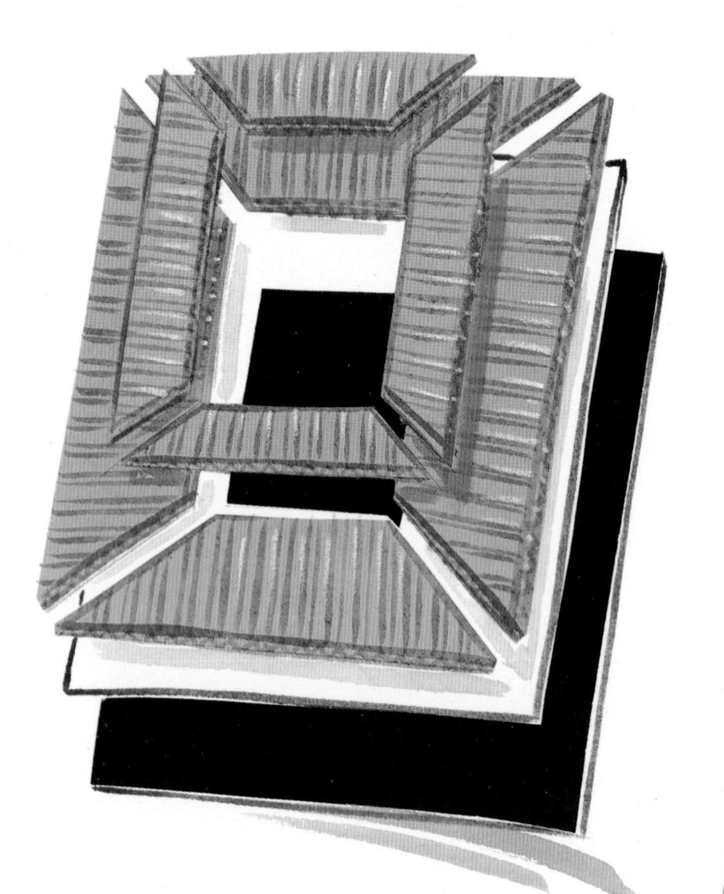

Card Frames

Rugged corrugated paper makes attractive and robust frames for snapshots and postcards. First make a base frame from stiff card to the required dimensions. Then cut strips of corrugated paper to fit on top, mitering the corners. Finally add an inner frame, cut to half the depth of the base, and stick on top to create the effect of molding. The completed frame can be painted, sprayed, or decorated – but looks equally good left untouched (left and below)**.**

Variations

Different versions of the same paper frame can be made by adding cut-out shapes. As before, make a plain card base and then cut out a frame from corrugated paper to match, gluing it on top. Apply chunky squares at each corner (above) **or cut out circles to stick on top for a bold sculptural effect** (left)**.**

The same general principles for displaying objects and collections also apply to picture hanging. You can group similar types of work – black-and-white prints or photographs, watercolors, and so on – to increase their effectiveness, or assemble a collection of pictures related by theme, such as animal prints or images of food and drink for a kitchen.

When hanging a group of pictures, one useful tip is to lay them out on the floor or on a table top to experiment with positioning. Symmetry can be a good idea if all the pictures are the same size, although assymetrical arrangement leaves open the possibilty of adding to the collection at a later date. You don't have to restrict yourself to traditional locations, such as above the fireplace. Emphasize a doorway by hanging small prints to follow the outline of the architrave or run a low horizontal line of pictures over a sofa for Neoclassical elegance. Stairways and halls are good places for dense picture hanging.

Original frames lift even the humblest photocopy out of the ordinary. Flea markets can be a good source of old, interesting frames, or you can decorate plain wood surrounds by painting or sticking on shells, stars, rope, or fabric. One quick framing idea is to build up borders using layers of corrugated paper, either sprayed or left natural. Fabric tape, rope, or ribbon are inventive ways of suspending pictures.

You can be just as eclectic in the selection of pictures you display. Prints of architectural detail, fresh from the photocopier, old photographs, collaged postcards, children's drawings – you don't have to patronize a gallery to find images that appeal to you.

FRAME IT

In The Frame

Customize old wooden frames with paint, mosaic, paper, stenciled detail, and fabric bows. Then use your imagination about what you put in the picture. Paint offers many possibilities: a square-ended brush dipped in black makes a checkerboard pattern on an ocher ground (above)**. Or you can cut a sponge into a squiggle shape and daub inky prints on a warm, tinted varnish base** (top left, main picture)**. Stick on paste jewels, or add**

bows of velvet, gauze, or gingham as a finishing touch to a plain frame (main picture)**. Torn scraps of paper can be pasted over a plain wooden frame** (right)**, while anise stars, sprayed gold, trim the four corners of a matt-black frame** (below)**. If you can't afford fine art, think laterally and display whatever catches your eye – photocopied prints artificially aged in tea or washed with varnish;**

sprayed leaves, pods, and spices; shells, labels, fabric swatches, and old family photographs can all form the basis for an imaginative and personalized picture collection.

LIGHTING

Lighting is a vital element in the design of space and one of the key factors contributing to that indefinable sense of atmosphere which forms the basis of successful decoration. Although you cannot radically alter lighting instantly, there are many ways of improving existing arrangements. Even on a tight budget there is a great deal you can do to create a better quality of light.

Make a start by reviewing the color and level of the light sources.Tungsten, the most common household light source, gives a warm, yellowish light which is easy on the eye and flattering to skin tones. On the other hand, fluorescent strip lighting (often found in kitchens) is unpleasantly green in tone. Its pallid glare, responsible for the sickly look of many institutional buildings, can make people look distinctly ill. Getting rid of fluorescent lighting, particularly the overhead variety, will improve your decoration at once.

Any overhead light, especially if the bulb is bright, throws an even glare over the room, obliterating shadows, flattening shapes and minimizing textural variety. You can improve matters greatly by dispensing with central fixtures in favor of individual points of light from table lamps or spotlights. These create atmospheric pools of light and shade, throw detail into relief and are every bit as effective in practical terms. And for economical, no-nonsense lighting it is hard to beat those versatile modern classics, the anglepoise lamp and the clip-on loft light, both stylish enough for living rooms, and also suitable for other lighting applications in the home.

There is a wide range of affordable lamps on the market, with plain ceramic bases in uncontroversial shapes and colors. Needless to say, these can be customized easily by sticking on stars, sequins, or anything that adds a little extra glitter and glamour. Lamp bases can also be painted to fit in with your overall color scheme or to stand out as a splash of interest. You can paint them using emulsion or enamel paints, or you could use special ceramic paints available from artists' suppliers. These are extremely easy to use and are "fired" in an ordinary oven, but do note that such paints should never be used on plates or other items intended for food use. Plain shades can also be decorated with paint, ribbon, or trimming, covered with patterned paper or fabric, or collaged with "found" materials or painted.

Striped Shade

Revamp a plain fabric lampshade with painted stripes (left)**. Trace around the outer and inner circumferences of the shade, marking the seam where the fabric joins. Divide the circles into sixteenths (less or more depending on how wide you want the stripes). Cut out the inner circle and place it on top of the shade, aligning one of the marked points with the seam; then place the bottom of the shade on top of the outer circle, again aligning one point with the seam. Next, transfer the marked points back onto the shade. Apply masking tape as shown, and then paint alternate segments into a contrasting color. When the paint is dry, remove the masking tape.**

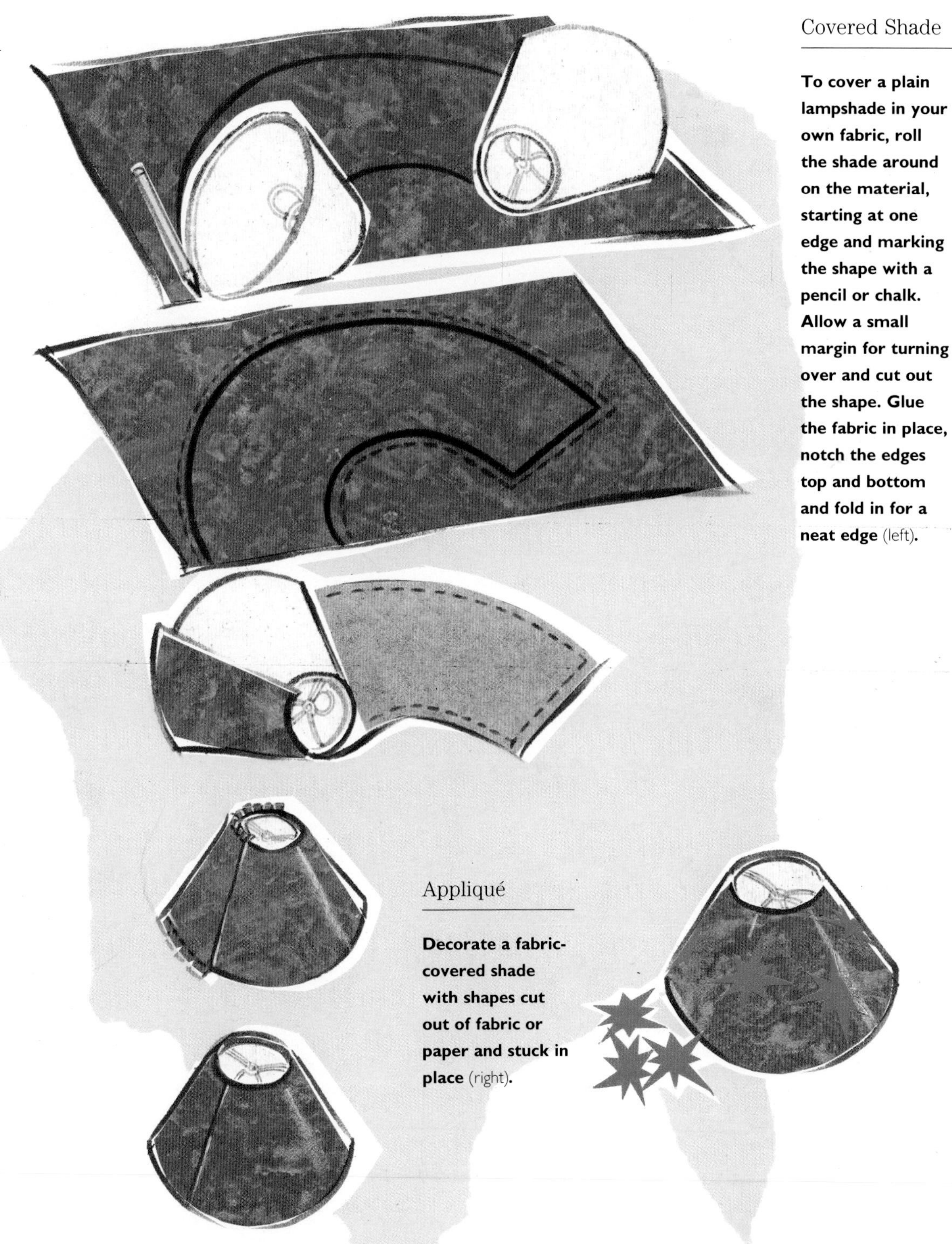

Covered Shade

To cover a plain lampshade in your own fabric, roll the shade around on the material, starting at one edge and marking the shape with a pencil or chalk. Allow a small margin for turning over and cut out the shape. Glue the fabric in place, notch the edges top and bottom and fold in for a neat edge (left)**.**

Appliqué

Decorate a fabric-covered shade with shapes cut out of fabric or paper and stuck in place (right)**.**

NATURE AT HOME

A cozy shelter. Eggs dressed in jewels. A lotus cup full of rainwater. A forest of tulips. Birds on the branch. Bring a bit of wonder home for the holidays.

FOR THE BIRDS

You never know when they might drop in for a visit. Treat these well-dressed guests to feeders, edibles and baths for the holidays.

F. LANTERN HUMMINGBIRD FEEDER
5¾"Dia. x 12"H. 897256 **$39**

G. COACH HOUSE FEEDER
8"Dia. x 11½"H. 897694 **$49**

H. CANOPY FEEDER
14"Dia. x 12½"H. 897033 **$69**

I. CERAMIC BIRDBATH
In Ivory, Aqua, Green (shown).
18"Dia. x 31½"H. 859751 **$149** ($10)

A
B
C
D

D

GLITTERING GIFTS

Hand-cut crystals capture light and turn it into sparkling jewels on holiday trees and gifts.

A. CRYSTAL HUMMINGBIRD, DRAGONFLY & FLOWER
Dragonfly 3½"H. 905950 **$20**
Hummingbird 3½"H. 905968 **$20**
Flower 3½"H. 905976 **$20**

B. CRYSTAL LOTUS FLOWER ORNAMENT
3"H. 905372 **$24**

C. CRYSTAL ORB GARLAND
9'7"L. 907436 **$24**

D. CRYSTAL GARLAND
6'L. 905364 **$36**

E. CRYSTAL SNOWFLAKES
(Set of 6.) 1½"Dia. 905356 **$18**

E

for the holiday hostess

STYLISH TRADITIONS

The scent of peppermint. A flickering votive. The wonder of snowfall in a globe. What new traditions do you want to start in your home?

H-I. KING LEO CANDY & COCOA
H. Peppermint Bark 1 lb. tin; 8¼"L x 6¼"W. 910091 **$20**

I. Hot Chocolate 1 lb. tin; 5¾"H. 910083 **$16**

J-L. RED LEAF MUGS, PLATES & TRAY
J. Mugs (Set of 4.) 8 fl. oz. 910117 **$30**
K. Plates (Set of 4.) 6¼"Sq. 910109 **$24**
L. Tray 13"L x 6½"W. 910125 **$18**

M. HOLIDAY VOTIVE CANDLEHOLDER
Glass; 3½"Dia. x 4½"H. 899617 **$6**

for the rustic spirit
NATURAL TREASURES
Bring some of nature's
most charming creations
home for the holidays.
A
B
C

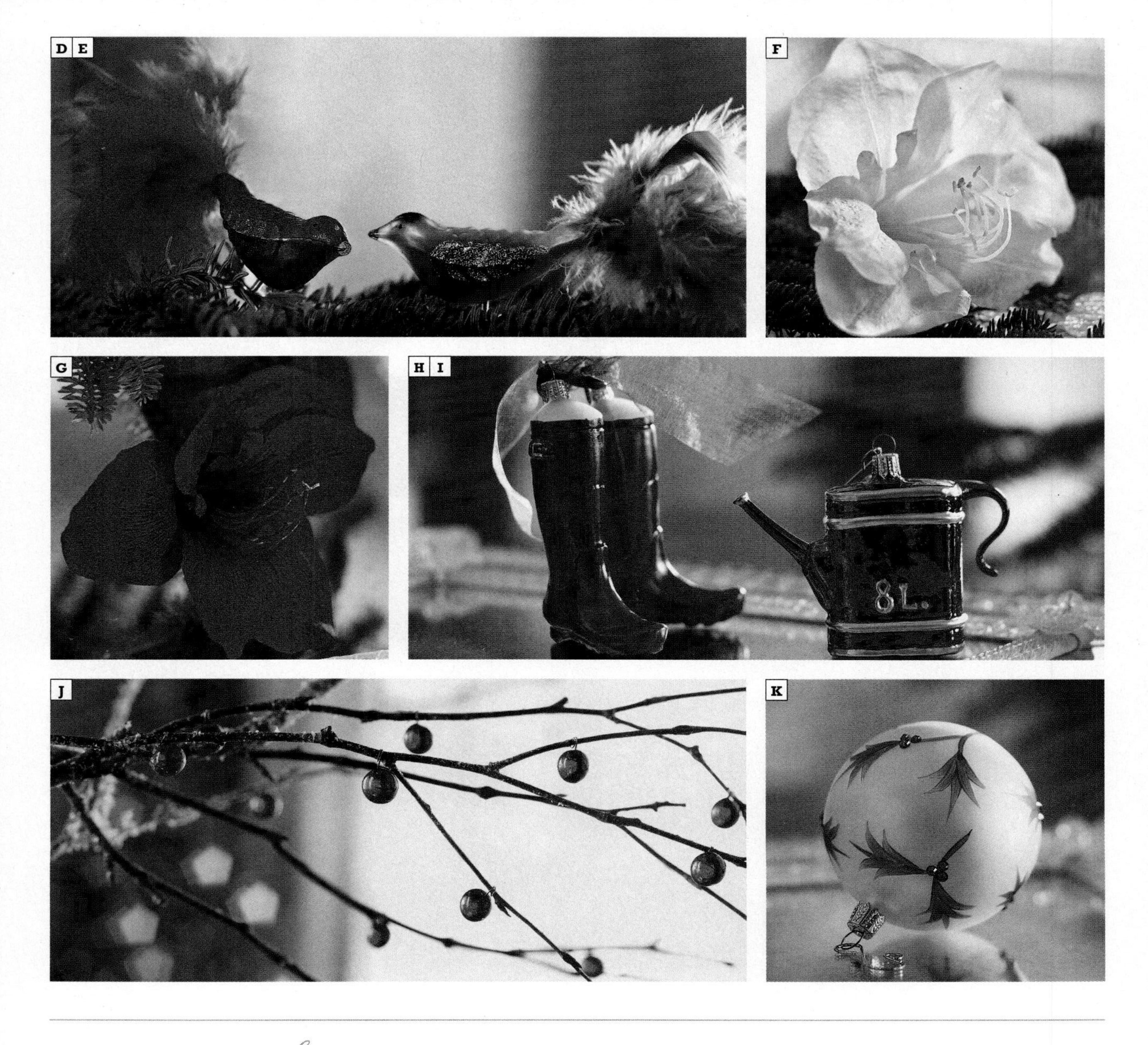
D E
F
G
H I
8L.
J
K

A

FLOWERS AND PLANTS

Containers

Hot Mexican colors transform garden plant pots into stylish containers for a collection of bristly cacti (left). **Fragile sweet pea flowers in plain glass containers, set on a sunny window sill form a bold but simple display in an instant** (right).

Canny retailers know that the tantalizing aroma of coffee or the smell of baking bread can stimulate well-being and freespending in their customers. Students of the property market advise that soft background music and fresh flowers in every room clinch more deals than the most fulsome realtor's prose. Such seemingly intangible factors play at subtle unconscious levels and greatly contribute to the overall sense of place.

Flowers bring life to the most clinical of surroundings. We instinctively appreciate some symbolic link with nature, even if it is just a straggling pot plant or a jug of spring daffodils. If you apply basic design sense in this area, too, you can make flowers and plants a more positive element in decoration.

As with any kind of display, scale is important. If fresh flowers represent a luxury item in your weekly budget, it is better to invest in a greater quantity of cheap flowers (generally those in season) which will have more impact than a few select blooms. Reflecting seasonal change through your choice of flowers is also a good way of bringing a sense of the outdoors closer to home.

Unless you have a well-stocked garden, free flowers mean wild-flowers which should be left alone to flourish. One exception is the hardy flowering species known as Queen Anne's lace, which is rampant in summer on wayside verges and waste-ground. The delicate white and fresh green of these flowers make excellent countrified arrangements, either on their own or combined with a few bought flowers. If you do have a garden, raid it regularly not just for flowers, but for foliage, berries, fall leaves and bare winter branches to supplement more traditional arrangements.

Containers for displays could not be easier to improvise. While a selection of jugs, vases, and plain glass containers are useful, galvanized buckets, watering cans, jam jars tucked inside baskets, and even test tubes have all been used to great effect by the more original floral designers. What counts is matching the style of the container to the quality of the flowers or foliage on display: delicate stems and fragile blooms in glass containers, spring bulbs in baskets or terra cotta pots, robust country bouquets spilling out of earthenware or enameled jugs.

Houseplants (as opposed to displays of cut flowers, foliage, or branches) have fallen from favor in fashionable circles in recent years. But whatever high style may decree, growing plants in containers will always be a satisfying and popular way of appropriating nature. The domestic charm of a row of bright geraniums on a sunny kitchen window sill, the dense tangle of fern fronds on a steamy bathroom ledge, or the dark trails of ivy tumbling over the side of a Welsh dresser will never disappoint. Truly exotic plants, such as succulents and cacti, are fascinatingly ugly, while herbs grown in containers are practical as well as beautiful.

Houseplants are best grouped together in locations which serve their needs. There are usually only a few sites around the home which can support plant life well, where light and warmth or moisture and shade are optimum for a particular family of plants. Happily, the needs of design and nature coincide: where conditions are right, fill the area with plants to make an impressive display. Stagger heights by combining hanging plants with plants on stands and at floor level. It is worth taking the time and trouble to decant plants from plastic pots into terra cotta ones, which can easily be "aged" by rubbing them with a little live yoghurt or unpasteurized milk to encourage the growth of lichen.

INDEX

Page numbers in *italic* refer to illustrations and captions

ACKNOWLEDGMENTS

The publisher would like to thank the following photographers and organizations for their permission to reproduce the photographs in this book:

6–7 Tim Street-Porter/Elizabeth Whiting and Associates; **8–10** above Tim Street-Porter; 10 below Roland Beaufre/Agence Top; **11** IPC Magazines/Robert Harding and Associates; **12–13** Margaret Courtney-Clarke; **14–15** Stylograph/Bayo; **16–17** ESTO/Mark Darley; **18** above IPC Magazines/Robert Harding Picture Library; **18** below Paul Ryan; **18–19** IPC Magazines/Robert Harding Picture Library; **20** Paul Ryan; **20–1** David Brittain/Metropolitan Home; **22** above Stylograph/P.Isla/Casa de Marie Claire; **23** left Fritz von der Schulenburg (Richard Hudson); **23** right Peter Woloszynski/Elizabeth Whiting and Associates; **29** Bruant/Puech/Postic/Marie Claire Maison; **30–1** Chabaneix/Bayle/Marie Claire Maison; **31** right Shona Wood (designer: Georgina Godley); **36** Michael Dunne/Elizabeth Whiting and Associates; **37** right Bailhache/Comte/Marie Claire Maison; **37** left Hussenot/Roy/Comte/Marie Claire Maison; **38** IPC Magazines/Robert Harding Picture Library; **39** left Stylograph/Olivier de Lerins/Côté Sud; **39** right Tim Street-Porter/Elizabeth Whiting and Associates; **40** Chabaneix/Bastit/Maire Claire Idées; **41** IPC Magazines/Robert Harding Picture Library; **42** left Camera Press; **42** right Ianthe Ruthven; **46–7** Stylograph/Ingalill Snitt/Côté Sud; **48–9** Roland Beaufre/Agence Top; **50–1** IPC Magazines/Robert Harding Picture Library; **55** IPC Magazines/Robert Harding Picture Library; **58–9** IPC Magazines/Robert Harding Picture Library; **66** Jean-Pierre Godeaut; **67** Christian Sarramon; **70** Christian Sarramon; **71** IPC Magazines/Robert Harding Picture Library; **72–3** Stylograph/Samcassani; **74** IPC Magazines/Robert Harding Picture Library; **77** Christian Sarramon; **80** Di Lewis/Elizabeth Whiting and Associates; **81** Christian Sarramon; **88–9** Chabaneix/Marie Claire Idées; **92** Nadia Mackenzie; **93** IPC Magazines/Robert Harding Picture Library; **96** left Victor Watts/Elizabeth Whiting and Associates; **96–7** Chabaneix/Chabaneix/Bastit/Marie Claire Idées; **102–3** IPC Magazines/Robert Harding Picture Library; **104** left Chabaneix/Bayle/Marie Claire Maison; **104–5** Nadia Mackenzie; **105** right Camera Press; **108** left Stylograph/B.Touillon/Côté Sud; **108** right Morel/Puech/Marie Claire Maison; **109** Chabaneix/Chabaneix/Bastit/Marie Claire Idées; **110** Stylograph/B.Touillon/Côté Sud; **111** IPC Magazines/Robert Harding Picture Library; **114** above left Camera Press; **114–5** Gilles Guerin/Agence Top; **124** Nadia Mackenzie; **125** Di Lewis/Elizabeth Whiting and Associates.

SPECIAL PROJECTS

The projects on the following pages were devised and specially photographed for Conran Octopus: 2, 4–5, 22 below, 24–5, 28, 32–3, 43, 52–3, 54, 57, 60–1, 64–5, 68–9, 75, 76, 78–9, 82–3, 84–5, 86–7, 90–1, 94–5, 106–7, 113, 114 below left, 115 right, 118–9, 122–3.

Art Direction *Claire Lloyd*
Photography *Richard Foster*
Photographic Assistant *Hannah Lewis*
Art Director's Assistant *Tiffany Davies*
Set Building *Jon Self*